Love
Stitching

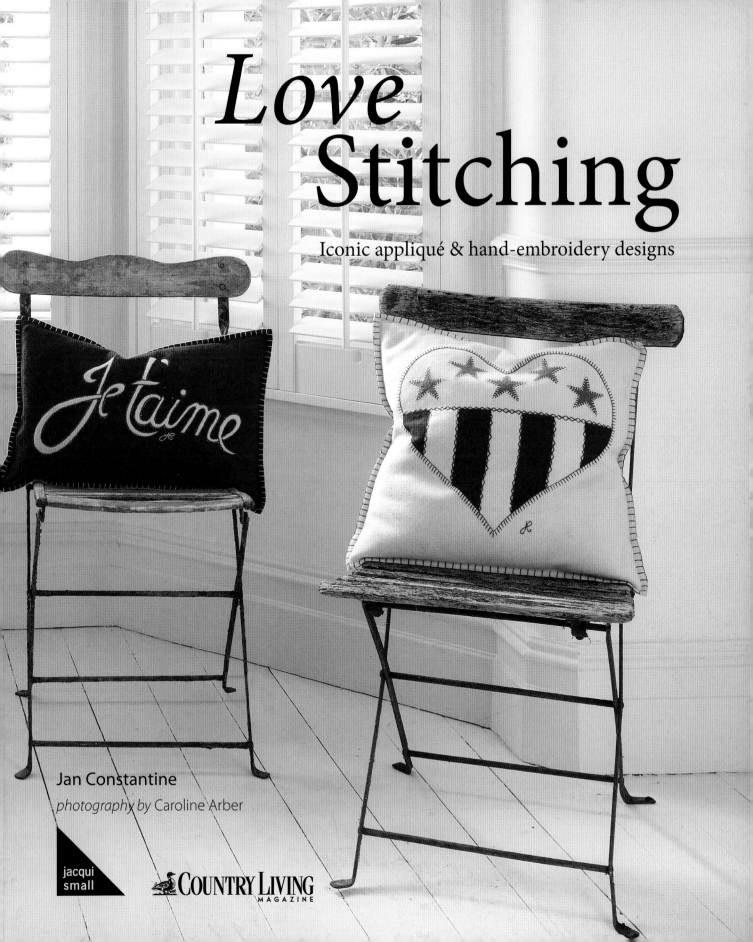

Love
Stitching

Iconic appliqué & hand-embroidery designs

Jan Constantine

photography by Caroline Arber

jacqui small

COUNTRY LIVING
MAGAZINE

Dedicated with love to my
grandmother, Mary Constantine.

First published in 2011 by **Jacqui Small LLP**
An imprint of Aurum Press Ltd
7 Greenland Street
London NW1 0ND

ISBN: 978 1 906417 53 6

A catalogue record for this book is available
from the British Library.

2013 2012 2011
10 9 8 7 6 5 4 3 2 1

Printed in China

Publisher Jacqui Small
Managing Editor Kerenza Swift
Commissioning Editor Zia Mattocks
Art Director Barbara Zuñiga
Illustrator Kate Simunek
Production Peter Colley

Contents

Introduction

Love is often referred to as the international language, overriding cultural and linguistic divisions. The love of stitching has been practised all over the world for centuries, and from one generation to the next, these valuable skills have been passed down and have flourished.

With this book, I hope to inspire new generations of stitchers – both those who have never stitched before and those who are experienced stitchers – to create something that will be cherished.

I learned to stitch at an early age from my mother and grandmother, who were my biggest sources of inspiration and who passed their creative genes and their love of stitching on to me. They always had wonderful projects on the go and between them made the most fashionable clothes, hats and furnishings.

Opposite Blanket stitch is a key component of my designs (see the Glossary of Stitches on page 140). I use it to outline appliqué shapes and to edge everything from cushions to throws. The gorgeous, bright pink Love Throw features cream appliqué hearts and the word 'love' in several languages. The shapes are outlined with blanket stitch worked using pink embroidery thread, while the throw itself is edged with the same stitch in cream.

Left The contrasting heart on the cute Heart Needle Case is made by reverse appliqué, where the outline is cut out from the main cover and a contrasting shape is appliquéd onto the reverse and then blanket stitched in the same colour.

I began by making clothes for my dolls and later I made all my own clothes. When I left school, I decided to follow my heart and went on to study fashion. I loved to create colourful and vibrant collections, and from those early student days embroidery was a strong feature of my work. I'll never forget those exciting trips to the wonderful fabric department at Liberty of London, where I would spend hours stroking the rolls of chintz and remnants of lawn cloth before spending my precious budget.

After graduating, I spent a decade working in London as a successful dress designer for a large company, and my collections were recognized for their appliqué, beading and embroidery detail. After moving to the Cheshire countryside, I established an interiors business and also styled for magazines and advertisement campaigns in London.

Yearning to work with textiles again, and with the encouragement of my friends and family who loved the creations I gave them, I started my business in 2002. My first collections were created around the kitchen table, where I sewed countless lavender hearts with the help of willing friends – and the occasional bottle of wine. Now, nine years later, my designs for cushions, bags, throws, wall hangings and other home furnishings and accessories have evolved and become recognized and collected worldwide.

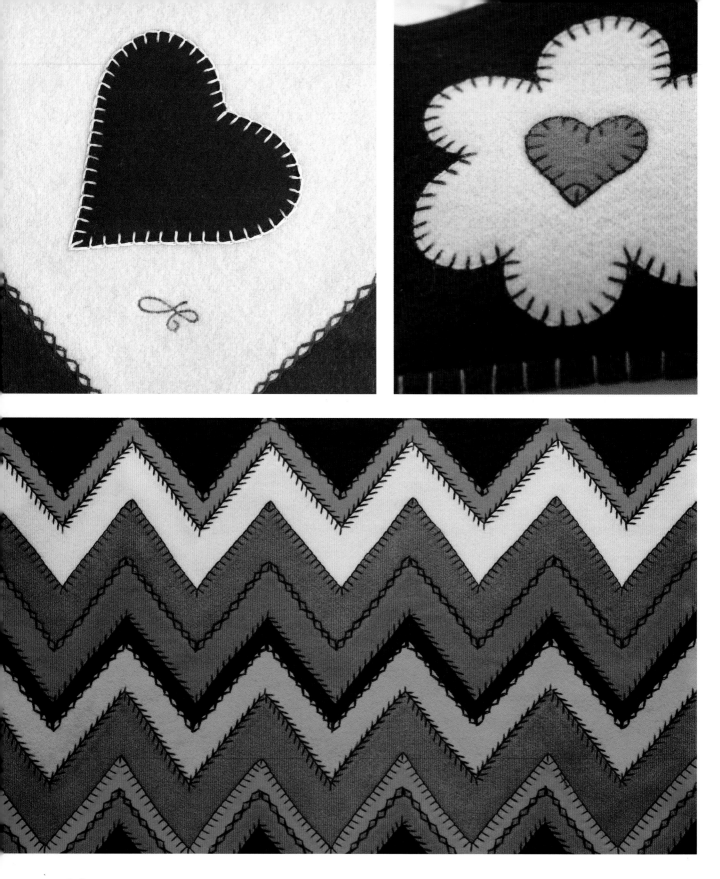

When designing my collections I go with my instincts and create what excites me. Colour is something that I've never been afraid of and I take great delight in using bright and contrasting colours for my bold appliqué embroideries. Remaining true to my heart has created my unique design DNA and this, mixed with hard work and total commitment, has made my name into a brand that is developing into many exciting products.

This book is filled with an eclectic mix of projects that are truly me – strong shapes, bold colours and exciting designs. Some are easy to make, while others need more experience.

The first chapter is called 'Love & Hearts', two words that epitomize my work and are the rocks of my business. As an eleven-year-old, I remember stitching beautiful, appliqué, red velvet hearts onto my blue tee-shirt and shorts.

In the country, where I live most of the time, I am inspired every day by the natural beauty that surrounds me. My second chapter celebrates and captures the wonderful things I see – from flowers to insects.

'Flying the Flag' uses the pure, graphic lines and strong colours of flags from around the world as a springboard for the designs in this chapter. I love flags from all countries, as they are very powerful and symbolic. I have made them into cushions, tea cosies, wall hangings and hearts for years.

The final chapter, 'Beside the Sea', is inspired by subjects dear to my heart. When I look at these designs I think about my holidays on the Cornish coast of Britain and my time spent on Nantucket and Martha's Vineyard in the USA.

I hope you will love stitching the projects in this book as much as I have, and that you will pass on your work as heirlooms, just as our ancestors passed on the heirlooms they loved.

Jan Constantine

Opposite Simple, graphic shapes, such as hearts, flowers and stripes, can be arranged into endless configurations, combinations and colourways, with different stitching, such as cross stitch and closed fly stitch, as well as ubiquitous blanket stitch, depending on the look you require for your finished piece.

Below The Lips Cushion is a bold and bright design that is really simple to make, once you have mastered blanket stitch, but stunning to look at.

Love & Hearts

Love Throw

This gorgeous, deep pink throw is appliquéd with the word 'Love' in five different languages – English, French, Spanish, Italian and German. A striking statement piece, it is a very easy project to sew using the simple blanket-stitch technique. The throw could be made as a gift and customized with other meaningful words or a different colour combination.

Embroidery stitches

Blanket stitch appliqué for the words and hearts, and blanket stitch edging (see page 140).

Preparation

Prepare the wool fabric by pressing (see tips on page 105).

Using a photocopier, enlarge the 'Love' words, printed in reverse on pages 109 and 110, by 250 per cent; the heart template is shown on page 109 at full size.

CUTTING OUT Referring to the notes on page 106, cut the throw to size from a length of pink wool felt. This throw is 160cm (63in) long and has been cut out from the whole width of the fabric (130cm/51in), with the selvedges trimmed off.

Appliqué

Referring to the bonding-web technique on page 105 and following the manufacturer's instructions, trace each of the five words and three hearts onto the bonding web using a sharp pencil (see picture 1). The letters must be traced onto the bonding web in reverse, so that they will be the right way around when the bonding web has been fused to the back of the fabric and the shapes have been cut out.

Iron the bonding web onto the wrong side of the contrasting cream wool felt (see picture 2).

Materials and equipment

160cm (63in) of pink wool felt (minimum width 130cm/51in) for the throw

40cm (16in) of cream wool felt for the 'Love' word and heart motifs

100 x 40cm (39 x 16in) of bonding web

'Love' words and heart templates (pages 109–10)

Throw diagram (page 108)

Sharp, hard pencil

Embroidery kit and stranded cotton embroidery thread (dyefast) in bright pink and cream

Sewing machine, matching thread and sewing kit

Iron and ironing cloth

1

2

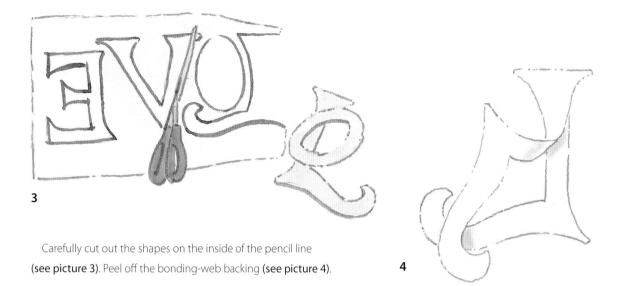

3

Carefully cut out the shapes on the inside of the pencil line (**see picture 3**). Peel off the bonding-web backing (**see picture 4**).

4

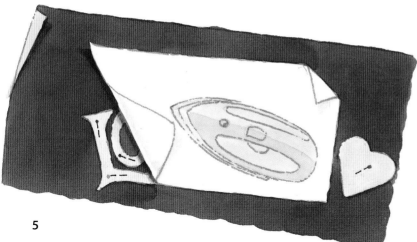

5

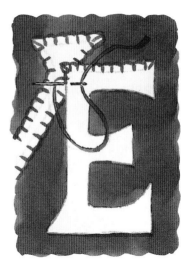

6

Referring to the diagram on page 108, pin the words and hearts, right side up, onto the right side of the throw, positioning each motif and overlapping the letters as shown. Using an ironing cloth between the hot iron and the wool fabric to protect it, iron to fuse the words and hearts to the throw (see picture 5).

EMBROIDERY Using four strands of pink embroidery thread, work blanket stitch neatly around the outline of the letters and hearts, sewing small stitches about 5mm (¼in) long and spacing them 5mm (¼in) apart (see picture 6).

Making up the throw

Fold the top and bottom edges of the throw 12mm (½in) to the wrong side, and pin and tack in place. To mitre the corners, fold the corners in neatly to form a right angle (see picture 7). Then fold the sides 12mm (½in) to the wrong side, and pin and tack in place. Machine stitch the hem all around the throw, then sew another parallel line of machine stitching along the very edge.

EMBROIDERY Using six strands of cream embroidery thread, work blanket stitch around the edge of the throw, using the machine-stitched lines as a guide and spacing the stitches 1cm (½in) apart (see picture 8).

Finishing

Press the throw lightly using a damp cloth between it and the iron to protect the fabric and prevent it from becoming shiny.

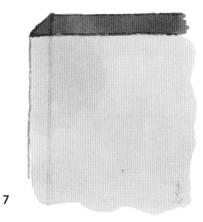

7

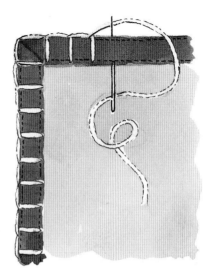

8

Lips Cushion

The bold, red lips motif on this cream oblong cushion is as simple as it gets in appliqué terms and is a perfect project for a novice to try. Given pride of place on a chair, in the centre of a sofa or on a bed, this lovely scatter cushion will always bring a smile.

Embroidery stitches

Blanket stitch appliqué and blanket stitch edging (see page 140), plus buttonhole stitch for the buttonholes (see page 141), or use the sewing machine.

Preparation

Prepare the wool fabric by pressing (see tips on page 105).

Using a photocopier, enlarge the front cushion pattern with the lips motif and the back cushion and facing patterns by 220 per cent.

TRACING THE DESIGN When the design is not symmetrical, as here, it needs to be traced in reverse before being traced through the bonding web, or the motif will appear the other way around on the finished cushion. Using a sharp pencil and tracing paper, trace the full-size lips motif in reverse onto a sheet of paper.

CUTTING OUT Referring to the notes on page 106, cut out one cushion front and two cushion backs in cream wool felt. Cut out two back facings in cotton and two in iron-on interfacing.

Appliqué

Following the bonding-web instructions for the Love Throw (see page 12), trace the reversed lips motif onto the bonding web with a sharp pencil.

Iron the bonding web onto the wrong side of the red wool felt and cut out the lip shapes inside the pencil line (**see picture 1**). **1**

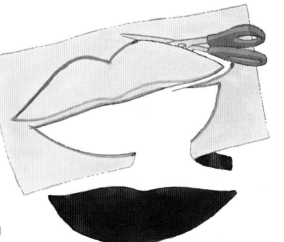

Materials and equipment

34 x 50cm (13½ x 20in) feather cushion pad

50cm (20in) of cream wool felt (minimum width 130cm/51in) for the cushion cover

40 x 20cm (16 x 8in) of red wool felt for the lips motif

Two 4 x 36cm (1¾ x 14in) pieces of cream cotton fabric for the back opening facings

40 x 20cm (16 x 8in) of bonding web

10 x 40cm (4 x 15¾in) of iron-on interfacing

Two buttons, 2cm (¾in) diameter

Front cushion pattern with lips motif template (page 112)

Back cushion and facing patterns (page 115)

Tracing paper and sheet of paper

Sharp, hard pencil

Embroidery kit and stranded cotton embroidery thread (dyefast) in cream and red

Sewing machine, matching thread and sewing kit

Iron and ironing cloth

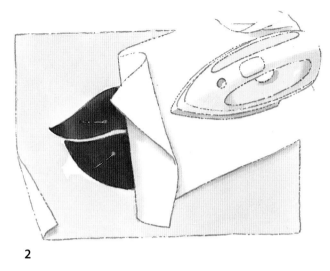

2

3

4

Peel off the bonding-web backing and pin the lips onto the centre of the cushion front, right sides up. Using an ironing cloth between the hot iron and the wool fabric to protect it, iron to fuse the lip shape to the cushion front **(see picture 2)**.

EMBROIDERY Using four strands of cream embroidery thread, outline the lips with blanket stitch sewing small stitches about 5mm (¼in) long and spacing them 5mm (¼in) apart **(see picture 3)**.

Making up the cushion

BACK FACINGS Using the iron, press iron-on interfacing to the wrong side of the cotton back facings. Turn one long edge of each facing under by 1cm (½in) and press the hems in place **(see picture 4)**.

With right sides together, pin and tack the other long edge of each facing to one of the wool felt cushion back pieces, then machine stitch the 1cm (½in) seams **(see picture 5)**.

Press the seams open and then fold the facings back onto the wrong side of the cushion backs and press. Pin, tack and machine a line of stitching 3.5cm (1½in) from the edge to hold each facing in place. Machine two parallel lines of stitching, one along each edge and the other 1cm (½in) in from the edge **(see picture 6)**.

BUTTONHOLES Mark two buttonhole positions on the wrong side of the right cushion back piece, positioning them 2cm (¾in) in from the edge and 12cm (4¾in) apart. Work two 2.5cm (1in) buttonholes by machine or by hand.

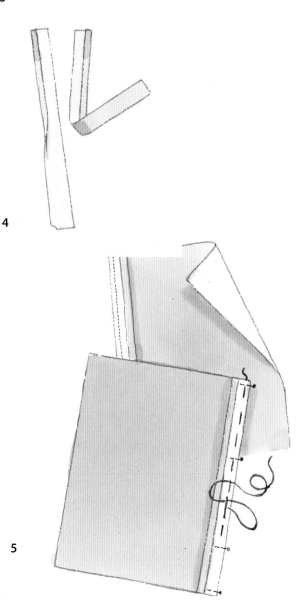

5

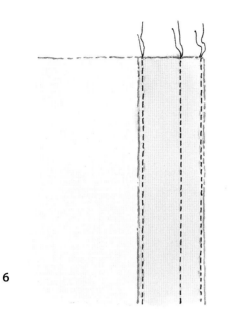

6

7

EMBROIDERY On the right back piece, work blanket stitch along the edge of the opening with six strands of red embroidery thread, using the inner machine-stitched line as a guide and spacing the stitches 1cm (½in) apart **(see picture 7)**.

Lay the right back piece over the left back piece, matching up the balance points at the top and bottom. Sew two buttons onto the left cushion back at the marked points, corresponding with the buttonholes on the right back piece.

Do up the buttons and tack the two pieces of the cushion back together at the top and bottom to secure **(see picture 8)**.

JOINING THE FRONT AND BACK With wrong sides together, pin the front and back of the cushion together, then tack and machine stitch 1cm (½in) seams around all four edges. Machine a parallel stitch line along the outer edge of the cushion.

EMBROIDERY Finally, press flat and trim the edges of the fabric, if necessary, to neaten. Using six strands of red embroidery thread, edge the cushion with blanket stitch. Work neat stitches using the inner stitch line as a guide and space them 1cm (½in) apart **(see picture 9)**.

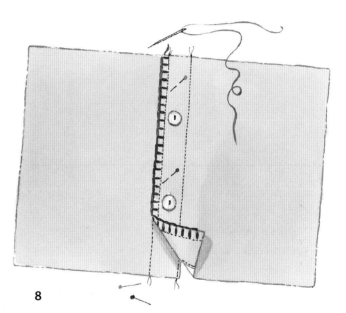

8

Finishing

Lightly press the finished cushion cover with a slightly damp cloth between the hot iron and the fabric to prevent it from becoming shiny.

Insert the cushion pad and do up the buttons.

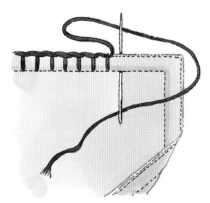

9

Heart Needle Case

This delightful needle case was inspired by a faded, old, green one that I have always cherished. I redesigned it and stitched a pink heart onto the front by reverse appliqué to produce the most exquisite little place to keep needles. The same technique can be used to make a gorgeous cushion cover (seen in the photograph on page 13) – use the basic pattern for the Stars & Stripes Heart Cushion (see pages 128–9).

Embroidery stitches

Blanket stitch appliqué and blanket stitch edging (see page 140).

Preparation

Prepare the wool fabric by pressing (see tips on page 105).

Using a photocopier, enlarge the pattern for the lining and outer cover with the heart motif by 150 per cent. Enlarge the pattern for the two inner pages by 150 per cent.

CUTTING OUT Referring to the notes on page 106, cut out one needle-case cover in cream wool felt. Using dressmaker's carbon paper between the fabric and the pattern (see page 106), held in place with masking tape, trace around the smaller heart template to transfer it onto the centre of the needle-case front cover, on the wrong side of the fabric. Carefully cut out the heart shape.

Using the larger heart template, cut out one heart shape in pink wool felt for the appliqué **(see picture 1)**.

Using pinking shears, cut out the inner pages – one large and one small – in cream wool felt.

Cut out one inside-cover lining in pink cotton.

Materials and equipment

- 15 x 60cm (6 x 23½in) of cream wool felt for the needle-case cover and inner pages
- 10 x 10cm (4 x 4in) of bright pink wool felt for the heart
- 15 x 25cm (6 x 9in) of bright pink cotton fabric (dyefast) for the lining
- 25cm (9in) of bright pink ribbon, 7mm (¼in) wide
- Needle-case pattern and heart motif template (page 116)
- Dressmaker's carbon paper
- Masking tape
- Embroidery kit and stranded cotton embroidery thread (dyefast) in bright pink
- Sewing machine, matching thread and sewing kit
- Pinking shears
- Iron and ironing cloth

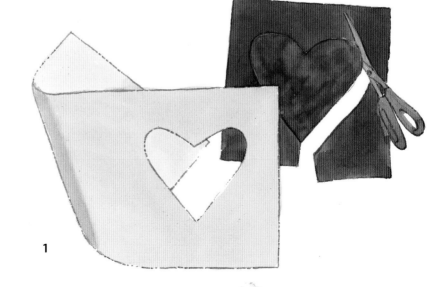

1

Appliqué

Position the right side of the pink heart against the wrong side of the corresponding cut-out heart shape on the needle case. Make sure the overlapping edges are even all the way around, and pin and tack the heart in position. Machine stitch the heart in place, sewing close to the cut-out edge on the front of the needle case in matching cream thread.

EMBROIDERY Starting at the top inverted point of the heart, work blanket stitch around the outer edge, using six strands of pink embroidery thread and making the stitches 5mm (¼in) long and spacing them 5mm (¼in) apart **(see picture 2)**.

When the embroidery is complete, iron lightly on the wrong side of the heart.

Making up the needle case

LINING With right sides facing, pin and tack the pink cotton lining to the cream felt needle case. Machine stitch with a 1cm (½in) seam all the way around, but leave a 6cm (2½in) gap on the back vertical edge of the needle case to turn it through to the right side **(see picture 3)**.

Trim the corners diagonally to remove bulk, remove the tacking and turn the needle case through to the right side, pulling the corners into shape. Neatly slip stitch the gap in the seam closed (see page 143) and then iron on the lining side of the needle case.

Machine stitch one row of topstitching close to the edge and then another row parallel to this 5mm (¼in) in from the edge.

EMBROIDERY Using six strands of pink embroidery thread, work blanket stitch all around the outside edges of the needle case, making the stitches 5mm (¼in) long and spacing them 5mm (¼in) apart.

RIBBON HOLES Using the sharp point of the scissors, carefully punch two holes, as marked on the needle-case pattern, through the centre of the cover and the two inner pages.

Finishing

Place the cream felt inner pages inside the needle case with the smaller rectangle on top, lining up the punched holes. To fasten the pages together, thread the pink ribbon through both holes from the inside of the needle case and tie in a bow in the centre of the outside of the spine **(see picture 4)**.

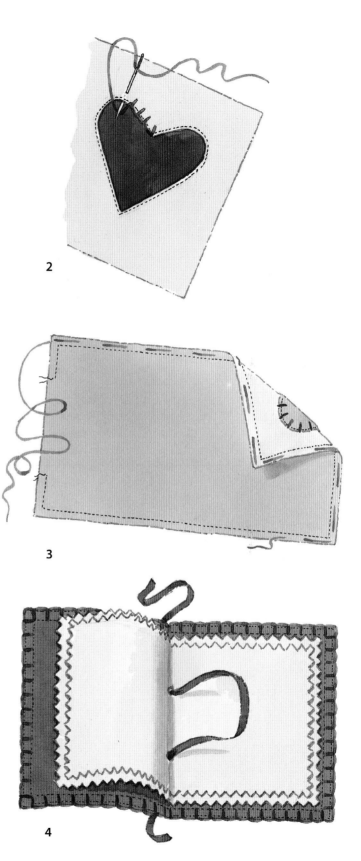

2

3

4

Floral Love Bag

This beautiful, black wool felt bag is embellished with the word 'love', appliquéd in contrasting red felt, and a burst of colourful embroidered flowers, which have been worked in chain stitch and French knots. It is just the right size to carry a few groceries or books, or to hang on a hook as a decorative accessory.

Embroidery stitches

Blanket stitch appliqué and blanket stitch edging (see page 140), chain stitch (see page 141) and French knots (see page 142).

Preparation

Prepare the wool fabric by pressing (see tips on page 105).

Using a photocopier, enlarge the bag pattern with the 'Love' motif and flower templates by 250 per cent. The 'Love' word, printed in reverse, is shown at full size.

CUTTING OUT Referring to the notes on cutting out on page 106, cut out one bag front and one bag back in black wool felt. Cut out one front and one back lining piece in red cotton.

Then cut out two facings in black wool felt measuring 42 x 6cm (16½ x 2⅜in). Cut out four handles in black wool felt measuring 38 x 3cm (15 x 1¼in).

Materials and equipment

30cm (12in) of black wool felt (minimum width 130cm/51in) for the bag

25 x 15cm (9 x 6in) of red wool felt for the 'Love' motif

30cm (12in) of red cotton fabric (dyefast, minimum width 130cm/51in) for the lining

25 x 15cm (9 x 6in) of bonding web

'Love' motif and flower templates (page 111)

Bag and lining pattern (page 111)

Dressmaker's carbon paper

Masking tape

Sharp, hard pencil

Embroidery kit and stranded cotton embroidery thread (dyefast) in red, blue, pink, yellow, purple, white, green and black

Sewing machine, matching thread and sewing kit

Iron and ironing cloth

Appliqué

Using dressmaker's carbon paper between the right side of the fabric and the template (see page 106), transfer the flowers and the position for the 'Love' motif onto the front piece of the bag **(see picture 1)**.

Following the bonding-web instructions for the Love Throw (see page 12), trace the outline of the word 'Love' in reverse onto a piece of bonding web using a sharp pencil.

1

2

Iron the bonding web onto the wrong side of the red wool felt. Carefully cut out the 'Love' motif on the inside of the pencil lines and peel off the bonding-web backing (**see picture 2**).

Pin the letters into position on the front piece of the bag. Using an ironing cloth to protect the wool felt from the hot iron, press with the iron to fuse the fabrics together.

EMBROIDERY Using four strands of red embroidery thread, blanket stitch neatly around the word 'Love', sewing small stitches 5mm (¼in) long and spacing them 5mm (¼in) apart.

Embroidering the flowers

Following the carbon-paper outlines and copying the colour combinations shown in the photograph on page 25, work the flowers in chain stitch and French knots using all six strands of thread from the skeins (**see picture 3**).

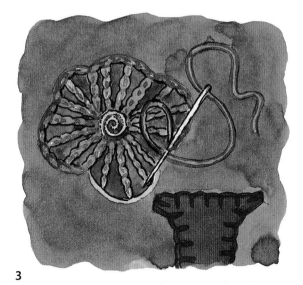

3

Making up the bag

Place the front and back pieces of the bag with right sides together and pin, tack and machine stitch a 1cm (½in) seam along both sides and along the bottom (**see picture 4**). Press the seams open.

GUSSET To form the gusset, with right sides together, arrange the bottom corners of the bag so that the seams at points A and B (as shown on the pattern) match and the edges are level. Tack and machine stitch 1cm (½in) seams across the corners of the bag base (**see picture 5**). Turn the bag right side out.

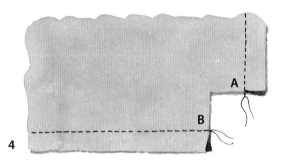

4

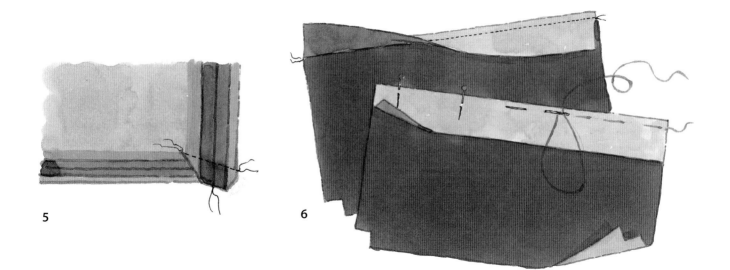

5

6

FACINGS With right sides together, pin, tack and machine stitch a 1cm (½in) seam to join the two bag facings to the top edges of the front and back pieces of the lining **(see picture 6)**. Press the seams open and overstitch the seam allowance to the wool felt. Make up the cotton lining in the same way as the bag.

HANDLES Place two black felt strips with wrong sides together and pin, tack and machine stitch a 1cm (½in) seam along both long edges. Then sew a parallel line of stitching close to the edges. Repeat for the second handle **(see picture 7)**.

Work blanket stitch using six strands of red embroidery thread along both sides of each handle, using the machine-stitched lines as a guide and spacing the stitches 1cm (½in) apart.

LINING Insert the lining into the bag with wrong sides facing each other. Slip the bag handles between the two layers of fabric at the marked balance points. Pin, tack and machine stitch a 1cm (½in) seam along the top edge and then sew a parallel line of stitching close to the edge **(see picture 8)**.

EMBROIDERY Finally, work blanket stitch around the top edge of the bag using six strands of red embroidery thread. Use the machine-stitched lines as a guide and space the stitches 1cm (½in) apart.

Finishing

Lightly press the finished bag (see notes on pressing and finishing on page 107).

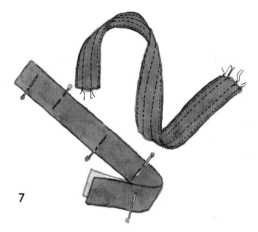

7

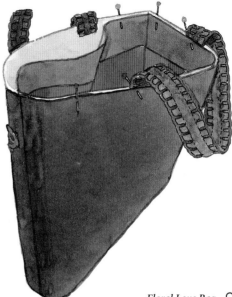

8

Multi-Heart Rug

This jolly little rug is perfect by the bedside and has been appliquéd with multiple red and pink hearts, and framed with a mitred pink border. The rug could easily be adapted to include different motifs, such as stars or daisies, or words, while the technique shown here could also be used to make a stunning, graphic, multi-heart cushion cover.

Embroidery stitches

Blanket stitch appliqué (see page 140) and cross stitch (see page 142).

Preparation

Prepare the wool fabric by pressing (see tips on page 105).

Using a photocopier, enlarge the rug border patterns by 350 per cent. The heart template is shown at full size.

CUTTING OUT Referring to the notes on cutting out on page 106, cut out one front rug panel in cream wool felt measuring 41.5 x 57.5cm (16³/₈ x 22¾in).

Using the rug border patterns, cut out one pair of the longer horizontal borders and one pair of the shorter vertical borders in pink wool felt.

Cut out one back lining in cream cotton fabric measuring 57.5 x 73.5cm (22¾ x 29in).

Appliqué

Referring to the bonding-web instructions for the Love Throw (see page 12), trace four hearts onto each piece of bonding web using a sharp pencil.

Iron one piece of bonding web onto the wrong side of the pink wool felt and the other onto the wrong side of the red wool felt.

Cut out the hearts neatly and peel off the bonding-web backing (see picture 1).

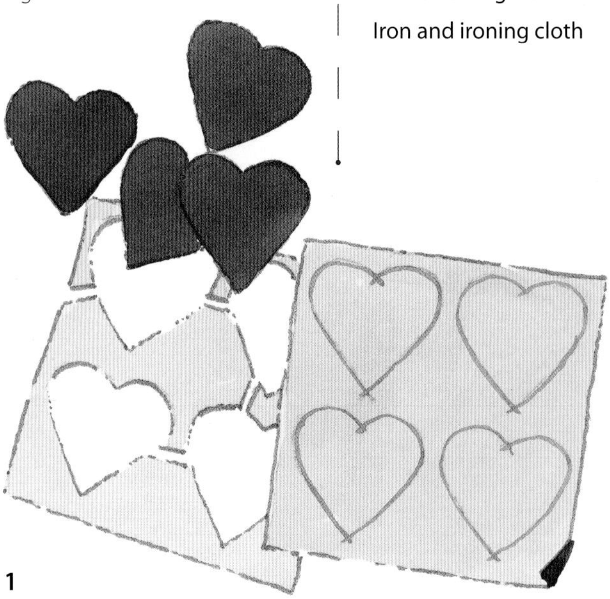

Materials and equipment

41.5 x 57.5cm (16³/₈ x 22¾in) of cream wool felt for the front rug panel

50 x 73cm (20 x 28¾in) of pink wool felt for the borders and hearts

25 x 25cm (9 x 9in) of red wool felt for the hearts

57.5 x 73.5cm (22¾ x 29in) of cream cotton fabric for the lining

Two 25 x 25cm (9 x 9in) pieces of bonding web

Rug diagram, border patterns and heart template (page 117)

Sharp, hard pencil

Tailor's chalk or marking pencil

Metal ruler

Embroidery kit and stranded cotton embroidery thread (dyefast) in cream and red

Sewing machine, matching thread and sewing kit

Iron and ironing cloth

1

2

Referring to the diagram on page 117, use a tape measure or ruler and tailor's chalk or a marking pencil to mark the positions for the red and pink hearts on the right side of the cream wool front panel. Pin the hearts in place, right sides up (**see picture 2**).

Using an ironing cloth between the hot iron and the wool fabric to protect it, iron to fuse the fabrics together.

EMBROIDERY Using six strands of cream embroidery thread, work blanket stitch around the outline of the hearts, sewing neat, even stitches about 5mm (¼in) long and spacing them 5mm (¼in) apart (see detail picture, opposite).

Making up the rug

BORDER Join the rug border pieces together at all four corners. Do this by placing the top and bottom bands together with the corresponding side bands at the corner mitres, with right sides together, and pin and tack in place (**see picture 3**).

Machine stitch the mitres with a 1cm (½in) seam allowance. Remove the tacking and press the seams open (**see picture 4**).

FRONT PANEL Lay the border out flat, right side up, and pin the front rug panel onto the border, matching the centre points and overlapping the border by 1cm (½in) all round. Pin and tack in place (**see picture 5**).

Thread the sewing machine with cream thread and machine stitch the cream front panel to the pink border, sewing along the cream edge all the way around.

3

4

5

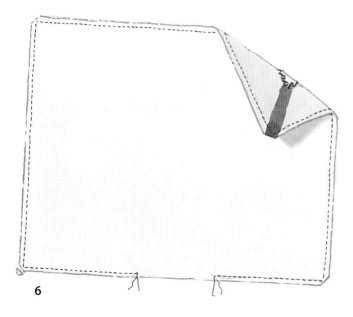

6

EMBROIDERY Using six strands of red embroidery thread, work cross stitch over the seam of the border and centre panel all the way around (see detail picture, right). Press carefully on the wrong side using an ironing cloth.

LINING Place the rug front and lining with right sides together and pin and tack all the way around the edge. Machine stitch a 1cm (½in) seam, leaving 10cm (4in) open in the centre of the bottom edge to turn the rug through. Using scissors, trim away the excess fabric on the corners of the rug to reduce bulk (**see picture 6**).

Turn the rug through to the right side and pull out the corners and edges evenly. Making sure the seam allowance is turned in at the opening in the bottom edge, press lightly on the wrong side of the rug.

TOPSTITCHING Thread the sewing machine with pink thread to match the border, and cream thread underneath to match the lining, then topstitch all the way around the edge of the rug, closing the opening in the bottom edge as you do so.

Finishing

Press the rug carefully using an ironing cloth.

Je t'aime Cushion

Saying 'I love you' in French always sounds so romantic and so chic. Sew this cushion for the loved one in your life, or indulge and stitch it for yourself, to add a romantic element to your boudoir or to adorn a favourite chair. It cannot fail to be a conversation piece and is a great way to add a bold splash of colour to a neutral décor.

Embroidery stitches

Zigzag chain stitch (see page 141) or small blanket stitch appliqué and blanket stitch edging (see page 140), plus buttonhole stitch for the buttonholes (see page 141), or use the sewing machine.

Preparation

Prepare the wool fabric by pressing (see tips on page 105).

Using a photocopier, enlarge the front cushion pattern with the 'Je t'aime' motif by 220 per cent. Enlarge the back cushion and facing patterns by 220 per cent. Using a sharp pencil and tracing paper, trace the full-size motif in reverse onto a sheet of paper.

CUTTING OUT Referring to the notes on page 106, cut out one cushion front and two cushion backs in red wool felt. Cut out two back facings in cotton and two in iron-on interfacing.

Appliqué

Following the bonding-web instructions for the Love throw (see page 12), trace the reversed 'Je t'aime' motif onto the bonding web using a sharp pencil (**see picture 1**).

Materials and equipment

34 x 50cm (13½ x 20in) feather cushion pad

50cm (20in) of red wool felt (minimum width 130cm/51in) for the cushion cover

40 x 20cm (16 x 8in) of cream wool felt for the 'Je t'aime' motif

Two 4 x 36cm (1¾ x 14in) pieces of red cotton fabric (dyefast) for the back opening facings

40 x 20cm (16 x 8in) of bonding web

10 x 40cm (4 x 15¾in) of iron-on interfacing

Two buttons, 2cm (¾in) diameter

Front cushion pattern with 'Je t'aime' motif template (page 113)

Back cushion and facing patterns (page 115)

Tracing paper and sheet of paper

Sharp, hard pencil

Embroidery kit and stranded cotton embroidery thread (dyefast) in cream and red

Sewing machine, matching thread and sewing kit

Iron and ironing cloth

1

2

Iron the bonding web onto the wrong side of the contrasting cream wool felt and carefully cut out the motif.

Peel off the bonding-web backing and pin the motif onto the centre of the cushion front piece, right sides up, as indicated on the pattern (see picture 2). Make sure the text is straight and, using an ironing cloth between the hot iron and the wool fabric to protect it, iron to fuse the motif to the cushion front.

EMBROIDERY Using four strands of red embroidery thread, outline the text with either zigzag chain stitch or small, neat blanket stitch (see picture 3).

Making up the cushion

Make up the Je t'aime Cushion in the same way as the Lips Cushion (see pages 18–19), but use six strands of cream rather than red embroidery thread for the blanket stitching on the edge of the back opening and around the edges of the finished cushion cover.

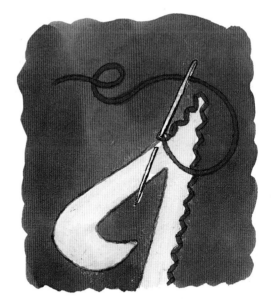

3

Finishing

Lightly press the finished cushion cover with a slightly damp cloth between the hot iron and the fabric to prevent it from becoming shiny.

Insert the cushion pad and do up the buttons.

In the Country

Ladybird Lavender Heart

This sweet little ladybird has been appliquéd and embroidered with satin stitch and chain stitch to create the most lovely hanging heart. It is filled with fragrant lavender, the relaxing scent traditionally used to keep linens smelling fresh and also to protect woollens from moths. You can hang it in your wardrobe or linen cupboard, or keep it out on display to add a decorative note to a bathroom or bedroom.

Embroidery stitches

Blanket stitch appliqué for the ladybird, blanket stitch edging for the heart edges (see page 140), satin stitch for the spots detail (see pages 142–3) and chain stitch for the legs and antennae (see page 141).

Preparation

Prepare the wool fabric by pressing (see tips on page 105).

Using a photocopier, enlarge the front heart pattern with the ladybird motif and the back heart pattern by 150 per cent.

TRACING THE DESIGN When the design is not symmetrical, as here, it needs to be traced in reverse before being traced through the bonding web, or the motif will appear the other way around on the finished heart. Using a sharp pencil and tracing paper, trace the full-size ladybird motif in reverse onto a sheet of paper.

CUTTING OUT Referring to the notes on page 106, cut out one 30 x 30cm (12 x 12in) piece of cream wool felt for the ladybird embroidery (this square is to be embroidered first and then cut into a heart shape for the front of the lavender heart using the pattern after the embroidery has been completed).

Using the heart back pattern piece, cut out two back pieces in cream wool felt to make up the heart shape.

Appliqué

Following the bonding-web instructions for the Love Throw (see page 12), trace the reversed body of the ladybird onto one piece of bonding web using a sharp pencil. Trace the head of the

Materials and equipment

30cm (12in) of cream wool felt for the heart

5 x 5cm (2 x 2in) of red wool felt for the ladybird's body

5 x 5cm (2 x 2in) of black wool felt for the ladybird's head

Two 5 x 5cm (2 x 2in) pieces of bonding web

40cm (16in) of cream silky cord, 4mm (1/8in) wide

Front heart pattern with ladybird motif template (page 118)

Back heart pattern (page 118)

Tracing paper and sheet of paper

Sharp, hard pencil

Dressmaker's carbon paper

Masking tape

15cm (6in) embroidery ring (optional)

Embroidery kit and stranded cotton embroidery thread (dyefast) in cream, black and red

Sewing machine, matching thread and sewing kit

80g (3oz) of fragrant loose lavender

Teaspoon to insert the lavender

Iron and ironing cloth

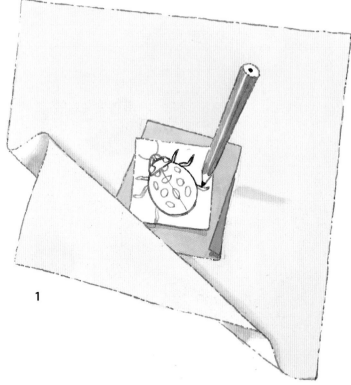

1

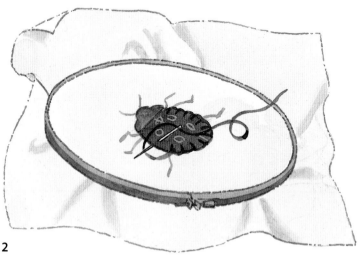

2

ladybird onto the other piece of bonding web. Iron the bonding web with the ladybird's body onto the wrong side of the red wool felt, and iron the bonding web with the ladybird's head onto the wrong side of the black wool felt.

Cut out the shapes neatly on the inside of the pencil lines and peel off the bonding-web backing. Pin the ladybird shapes in place, right side up, on the centre of the cream square. Using an ironing cloth between the hot iron and the wool fabric to protect it, iron to fuse the ladybird to the cream wool felt.

EMBROIDERY Using dressmaker's carbon paper between the right side of the wool felt and the design template (see page 106), trace over the ladybird's legs, eyes and spots to transfer the details of the design onto the felt (**see picture 1**).

Position the motif in the middle of a 15cm (6in) embroidery ring, stretching the felt taut. It isn't essential to use an embroidery ring, but it helps when there is fine detail to stitch.

Using four strands of black embroidery thread, work blanket stitch around the outline of the ladybird's red body and black

head, making the stitches 4mm (⅛in) long and spacing them 3mm (⅛in) apart (**see picture 2**).

For the legs, antennae and central line down the body that separates the wings, work chain stitch using three strands of black embroidery thread.

For the satin-stitch spots on the wings of the ladybird, use all six strands of black or cream embroidery thread accordingly (see detail picture, opposite).

When the ladybird embroidery is complete, remove the felt square from the embroidery ring and press lightly on the back (see notes on page 107).

Cut the front piece to size using the heart pattern.

Making up the lavender heart

SEWING UP THE BACK With right sides facing, pin, tack and machine stitch the central seam of the back heart pieces together, leaving a gap between the two balance points – this will be used to insert the lavender later (**see picture 3**). Press the seam open.

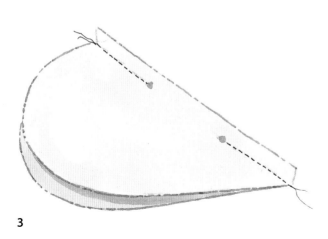

3

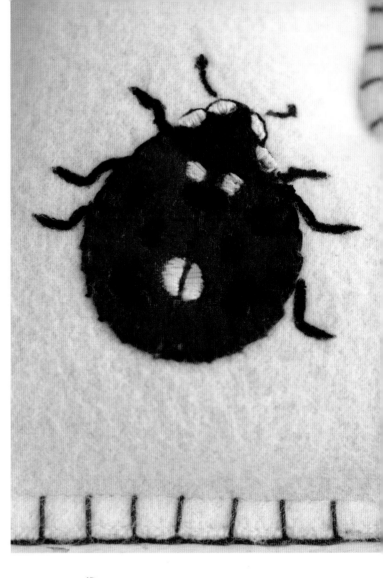

HANGING LOOP Lay the front of the heart right side down on the work surface and place the ends of the cord hanging loop in position on the balance points, so that the cord will hang from the top seam once the heart has been stitched together.

JOINING THE FRONT AND BACK With wrong sides facing, pin the front and back pieces of the heart together. Starting at the top centre of the heart, tack and then machine stitch around the edge of the heart with a 1cm (½in) seam allowance. Machine stitch another line on the outer edge, running parallel to the previous stitch line. Trim with scissors, if necessary, to tidy up the edges.

EMBROIDERY Starting at the centre top, work blanket stitches around the edge of the heart using six strands of red embroidery thread. Using the inner machine-stitched line as a guide, make the stitches 8mm (⅜in) long and space them 8mm (⅜in) apart.

Finishing

Lightly press the heart with a slightly damp cloth between the hot iron and the wool fabric to prevent it from becoming shiny.

Using a teaspoon, fill the heart with lavender (**see picture 4**).

Close the gap in the back seam with neat slip stitch (see page 143).

4

Butterfly Cushion

The majestic butterfly design, always a favourite motif, is based on the Red Admiral. Stitched with great patience, using tiny appliqué detail and French knots in a vibrant combination of dramatic black with deep pink, purple and cream, this cushion will be centre stage on any sofa or take pride of place in a boudoir.

Embroidery stitches

Blanket stitch edging (see page 140), zigzag chain stitch (see page 141), French knots (see page 142), satin stitch (see pages 142–3) and chain stitch (see page 141), plus buttonhole stitch for the buttonholes (see page 141), or use the sewing machine.

Preparation

Prepare the wool fabric by pressing (see tips on page 105).

Using a photocopier, enlarge the front cushion pattern with the butterfly motif template and the back cushion and facing patterns by 400 per cent. At full size, the wingspan measures 52cm (20½in).

CUTTING OUT Referring to the notes on page 106, cut out one cushion front and two cushion backs in pink wool felt. Cut out two back facings in pink cotton and two in iron-on interfacing.

Appliqué

The butterfly has many intricate markings and these areas need to be stitched onto the butterfly first, to avoid stitching through too many layers at once. Using dressmaker's carbon paper between the right side of the fabric and the butterfly motif template (see page 106), transfer the design onto the piece of black wool felt using a sharp pencil **(see picture 1)**.

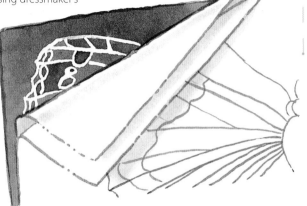

1

Materials and equipment

40 x 58cm (16 x 23in) feather cushion pad

50cm (20in) of bright pink wool felt (minimum width 130cm/51in) for the cushion cover

55 x 25cm (22 x 9in) of black wool felt for the butterfly

25 x 25cm (9 x 9in) of cream wool felt for the butterfly detail

Two 4 x 42cm (1¾ x 16½in) pieces of pink cotton fabric (dyefast) for the back opening facings

Two 50 x 25cm (20 x 9in) pieces of bonding web

10 x 45cm (4 x 17¾in) of iron-on interfacing

Two buttons, 2cm (¾in) diameter

Front cushion pattern with butterfly motif template (page 119)

Back cushion and facing patterns (page 119)

Sharp, hard pencil

Dressmaker's carbon paper

Masking tape

Embroidery kit and stranded cotton embroidery thread (dyefast) in black, purple and cream

Sewing machine, matching thread and sewing kit

Iron and ironing cloth

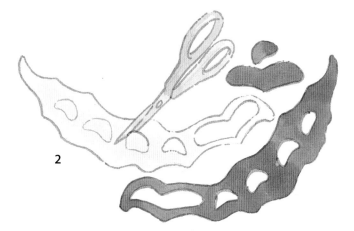

2

3

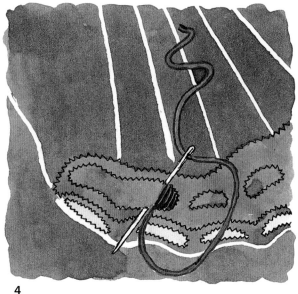

4

Following the bonding-web instructions for the Love Throw (see page 12) and referring to the photograph, trace the shapes of the butterfly's cream appliqué wing and head details onto one piece of bonding web using a sharp pencil. Trace the pink appliqué wing details onto another piece of bonding web in the same way.

Iron the corresponding pieces of bonding web onto the wrong side of the cream and pink fabrics and carefully cut out the small shapes, including the cutaway holes in the pink strip for the lower wings (see picture 2).

Peel off the bonding-web backing and, referring to the photograph on page 43, pin the shapes carefully, right side up, onto the correct areas of the black butterfly, as marked (see picture 3). Using an ironing cloth between the hot iron and the fabric to protect it, iron to fuse the shapes into position.

EMBROIDERY Using two strands of black embroidery thread, outline all the appliqué details with zigzag chain stitch.

Using three strands of purple embroidery thread, work chain or satin stitch to infill the areas as marked (see picture 4).

ATTACHING THE BUTTERFLY Using the iron, fuse bonding web to the back of the black wool fabric with the butterfly shape on it, then carefully cut around the outline of the butterfly and peel away the bonding-web backing.

5

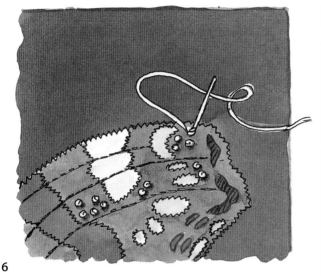

6

Position the butterfly shape in the centre of the pink cushion front and pin it in place. Using an ironing cloth, as before, iron to fuse it in position (**see picture 5**).

EMBROIDERY Using two strands of black embroidery thread, outline the butterfly with zigzag chain stitch.

Using three strands of black embroidery thread, work chain stitch to create the veins on the wings, the markings on the body and the antennae.

Infill the ends of the antennae in black satin stitch.

Finish with large, cream French knots on the upper wings, using all six strands of thread (**see picture 6**).

Making up the cushion

Make up the Butterfly Cushion in the same way as the Lips Cushion (see pages 18–19), but space the buttonholes on the right cushion back 14cm (5½in) apart rather than 12cm (4¾in), and use six strands of black embroidery thread rather than red for the blanket stitching on the edge of the back opening and on the edges of the finished cushion.

Finishing

Lightly press the finished cushion cover with a slightly damp cloth between the hot iron and the fabric to prevent it from becoming shiny.

Insert the cushion pad and do up the buttons.

Psychedelic Flowers Bag

Reminiscent of a fantastic, multicoloured printed dress that my mother sewed for me when I was a child, this fabulous psychedelic bag is a riot of glorious colour. It is made from overlapping patches, edged with a variety of embroidery stitches to create a wonderful work of art.

Embroidery stitches

Blanket stitch (see page 140), closed fly stitch (see page 143) and cross stitch (see page 142).

Preparation

Prepare the wool fabric by pressing (see tips on page 105).

Using a photocopier, enlarge the different coloured appliqué design templates printed in reverse on pages 122–3 by 150 per cent; the yellow appliqué elements are shown on page 121 at full size. Enlarge the bag and lining patterns by 250 per cent.

CUTTING OUT Referring to the notes on cutting out on page 106, cut out one bag front, one bag back, two zip gussets and one inside pocket in black wool felt. Cut out one front, one back and two zip-gusset lining pieces in bright pink cotton.

Cut out one black wool felt shoulder strap measuring 110 x 10cm (43 x 4in), using a ruler and tailor's chalk across the fabric width.

Appliqué

Using dressmaker's carbon paper between the right side of the fabric and the template (see page 106), trace the design onto the front bag piece.

Referring to the bonding-web instructions for the Love Throw (see page 12), trace the different coloured elements of the design onto separate pieces of bonding web. Iron the pieces of bonding web onto the wrong side of the corresponding coloured wool felt and cut out the shapes (**see picture 1**).

Materials and equipment

- 50cm (20in) of black wool felt for the bag
- 40cm (16in) of bright pink cotton fabric (dyefast, minimum width 90cm/35½in) for the lining
- 25 x 25cm (9 x 9in) each of green, pink, blue and orange wool felt for the appliqué design
- 15 x 15cm (6 x 6in) of yellow wool felt for the appliqué design
- Four 25cm (9in) squares and one 15cm (6in) square of bonding web
- 34cm (13½in) nylon zip
- 10cm (4in) of bright pink taffeta ribbon, 7mm (¼in) wide, for the zip pull
- Psychedelic flowers design templates (pages 121–3)
- Bag and lining patterns (pages 120–1)
- Dressmaker's carbon paper
- Masking tape
- Sharp, hard pencil
- Metal ruler
- Tailor's chalk or marking pencil
- Embroidery kit and stranded cotton embroidery thread (dyefast) in green, pink, blue, orange and yellow
- Sewing machine, matching thread and sewing kit
- Iron and ironing cloth

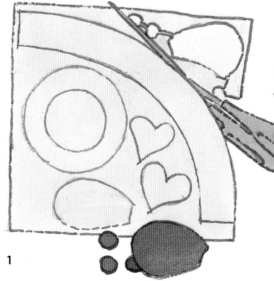

1

2

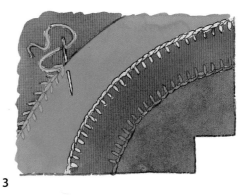

3

Some of these elements have areas of underlap (marked with slotted lines), which will fit under the adjacent motif in the design. This is to secure the appliqué shapes where the embroidery only holds down the edges.

BUILDING UP THE DESIGN Peel off the bonding-web backing and, following the design marked on the bag and referring to the photograph on page 47, start to pin the pieces in place, right side up on the front of the bag. Build up the design in sequence (as some of the pieces need to overlap others). Start with the orange ring, then overlap it with the pink ring by 5mm (¼in). Next, lay the large green ring edge to edge with the pink. Place the yellow circle in the middle of the orange ring and then lay the tiny pink circle on top. Using an ironing cloth between the hot iron and the wool felt to protect it, iron to fuse the shapes to the bag front.

Then apply the flower petals, with the upper orange petal first, overlapping the outer rings of the circle, then the rest of the petals in sequence, overlapping them according to the photograph (see picture 2).

Apply the rainbow next, starting with the large green arc that overlaps the flower petals. The pink arc sits edge to edge with the green and blue arcs, but the blue arc is overlapped by the small orange arc. Apply the central circles of the flower after the rainbow has been applied.

Apply the small circles on top of one another, with the yellow at the bottom, then the blue, and the pink in the centre on top.

Lastly, pin the two small pink hearts and the yellow star into position and fuse with the iron and ironing cloth as before.

EMBROIDERY Using a mixture of stitches in pink, blue, orange, green and yellow embroidery threads, outline the motifs as shown in the photograph. Use four strands of thread for the blanket stitch, making the stitches 5mm (¼in) wide and spacing them 5mm (¼in) apart. Use four strands of thread for the closed fly stitch, making the stitches 5mm (¼in) long and spacing them 5mm (¼in) apart (see picture 3). Use all six strands of thread for the cross stitch, making the stitches 1cm (½in) long and 5mm (¼in) wide.

Making up the bag

POCKET To make the inside pocket, first fold the facing to the wrong side and pin, tack and machine stitch close to the edge.

With wrong sides together, fold the pocket at the fold line and press. Pin and tack the pocket in position on the right side of the back bag lining, matching the balance points (see picture 4). Machine stitch along the two sides and bottom edge of the pocket, close to the edge, and then stitch a second parallel row 1cm (½in) away from the edge.

4

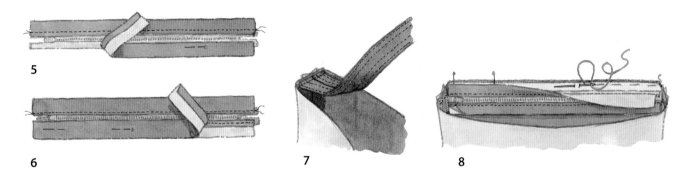

5

6

7

8

Place the front and back pieces of the bag with right sides together. Pin, tack and machine stitch the sides with a 1cm (½in) seam. Press the seams open. Repeat for the front and back lining pieces.

ZIP GUSSET Fold and press one long edge of the zip-gusset lining 1cm (½in) to the wrong side. Lay the zip wrong side up and pin and tack the folded edge to one side of the zip, with the lining right side up and the fold to the wrong side of the zip. Machine stitch in place, approximately 1cm (½in) from the centre of the zip teeth. Repeat to attach the other zip-gusset lining to the other side of the zip. Press the lining away from the zip teeth (**see picture 5**).

Turn the zip right side up. Fold one long edge of the wool felt gussets 1cm (½in) to the wrong side and press. Pin and tack the folded edge (with the fold underneath) on the front of one side of the zip, with the folded edge very close to the zip teeth. Making sure the lining is pressed out of the way, machine stitch in place, 5mm (¼in) from the folded edge. Repeat on the other side of the zip (**see picture 6**).

SHOULDER STRAP Fold the strip of fabric in half lengthways with right sides together. Pin, tack and machine stitch a 1cm (½in) seam down the long edge, leaving both ends open. Gently press the seam open, turn the strap through to the right side and press it flat with the seam in the centre of the strap. Machine stitch along both edges of the strap, then stitch a parallel row 1cm (½in) in from the edge on both sides. With right sides together, pin and tack the ends of the strap to the bag, positioning them between the balance points on either side of the top edge, and machine stitch in place (**see picture 7**).

ATTACHING THE ZIP GUSSET With right sides together, pin and tack the top edge of the bag to the zip gusset, matching the balance points and making sure the zip-gusset lining is folded back and out of the way (**see picture 8**). Snip into the seam

where the needle will pivot around the corners of the gusset to allow for movement, then machine stitch in place.

With the bag lining on the other side of the zip, pin, tack and then machine stitch the top edge of the bag lining to the zip-gusset lining in the same way, with right sides together.

Clip the corners of the gusset to reduce bulk, press and then open the zip by reaching through the unsewn bottom of the bag.

GUSSET With right sides together, pin, tack and machine stitch the bottom edges of the front and back bag pieces together. To form the bottom gusset, with right sides together, arrange the bottom corners so that the seams at points A and B (as shown on the pattern) match and the edges are level. Pin, tack and machine stitch a 1cm (½in) seam across both corners of the bag.

Repeat this for the bottom edge of the front and back lining, but leave a 15cm (6in) gap in the middle for turning the bag through (**see picture 9**).

Pull the bag right side out through the gap in the lining. Slip stitch the seam together (see page 143) and push the lining through the zip opening inside the bag.

Finishing

Lightly press the finished bag (see notes on page 107).

Loop the ribbon through the zip pull, fold the raw ends 1cm (½in) to the inside and stitch securely.

9

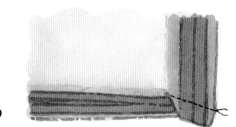

Daisy Make-Up Bag

With a 1960s vibe, this funky make-up bag featuring bold daisy and heart motifs is easy to embroider and can be adapted to carry pencils and pens, or made smaller as a money purse. It is a lovely project to make as a gift, and the colours can be changed as you wish, so it is the ideal way to use up scraps of wool felt left over from other projects.

Embroidery stitches

Blanket stitch appliqué, blanket stitch edging (see page 140) and zigzag chain stitch or buttonhole stitch (see page 141).

Preparation

Prepare the wool fabric by pressing (see tips on page 105).

Photocopy the pattern shown at full size on page 124.

CUTTING OUT Referring to the notes on cutting out on page 106, cut out one make-up bag front and one make-up bag back in black wool felt.

Cut out one front and one back lining piece in pink cotton.

Appliqué

Following the bonding-web instructions for the Love Throw (see page 12), trace the outline of the large daisy, medium heart and two tiny hearts on the zip pull onto one piece of bonding web, using a sharp pencil. Iron the bonding web onto the wrong side of the yellow wool felt.

In the same way, trace the medium daisy and large heart onto the other piece of bonding web and iron it onto the wrong side of the pink wool felt.

Carefully cut out all the motifs and peel away the bonding-web backing.

First, pin the pink daisy motif into position on the front piece of the bag, right sides up. Using an ironing cloth between the hot iron and the wool fabric to protect it, iron to fuse the fabrics together.

Next, pin the yellow daisy in place, slightly overlapping the pink daisy, and press in place as before (**see picture 1**).

Materials and equipment

20 x 20cm (8 x 8in) of black wool felt for the make-up bag and zip pull

10 x 10cm (4 x 4in) of yellow wool felt for the daisy and hearts

10 x 10cm (4 x 4in) of pink wool felt for the daisy and heart

20 x 20cm (8 x 8in) of pink cotton fabric (dyefast) for the lining

Two pieces of bonding web, 10 x 10cm (4 x 4in)

20cm (8in) nylon zip

10cm (4in) of pink ribbon, 7mm (¼in) wide, for the zip pull

Daisy and heart motif templates (see page 124)

Bag and lining patterns (see page 124)

Dressmaker's carbon paper

Masking tape

Sharp, hard pencil

Embroidery kit and stranded cotton embroidery thread (dyefast) in pink and black

Sewing machine, matching thread and sewing kit

Iron and ironing cloth

1

Add the contrasting hearts to the centre of each daisy in the same way.

EMBROIDERY Work blanket stitch neatly around the edge of the daisies and hearts using four strands of black embroidery thread, making small stitches 5mm (¼in) long and spacing them 5mm (¼in) apart.

DAISY ZIP PULL Fuse one tiny yellow heart onto the centre of each of the two small squares of black wool felt, right sides up, as described above. Work zigzag chain stitch or small neat buttonhole stitch around the edges of the hearts using three strands of pink embroidery thread.

Trace the outline of the small black daisy onto a piece of bonding web and iron it onto the wrong side of one of the squares of black wool felt with a yellow heart embroidered in place. Cut out the daisy shape and peel away the bonding-web backing.

Thread the piece of ribbon through the zip pull and lay the ends flat on top of each other on the wrong side of the black square, close to the bottom point of the heart (see picture 2).

With wrong sides together, pin the cut-out daisy on top of the black square, with the ends of the ribbon between the two layers and the bottom point of the heart towards the ribbon. Fuse the fabrics together, as before, and then cut carefully around the petals of the motif to create a double-sided daisy.

Using a needle and black cotton thread, topstitch the end where the ribbon is inserted for extra security (see picture 3).

Work blanket stitch neatly around the edge of the daisy zip pull using four strands of pink embroidery thread, making small stitches 5mm (¼in) long and spacing them 5mm (¼in) apart.

Making up the make-up bag

JOINING THE LINING TO THE ZIP With wrong sides together, turn over the top edge of the front and back lining pieces by 1cm (½in) and press in place.

Lay the folded edge of one lining piece, with right side facing up and the fold underneath, onto the back of one side of the zip. Make sure it is straight and flat with the folded edge 2mm (¹⁄₁₆in) from the teeth. Pin, tack and then machine stitch close to the edge of the fold, using a zipper foot on the sewing machine.

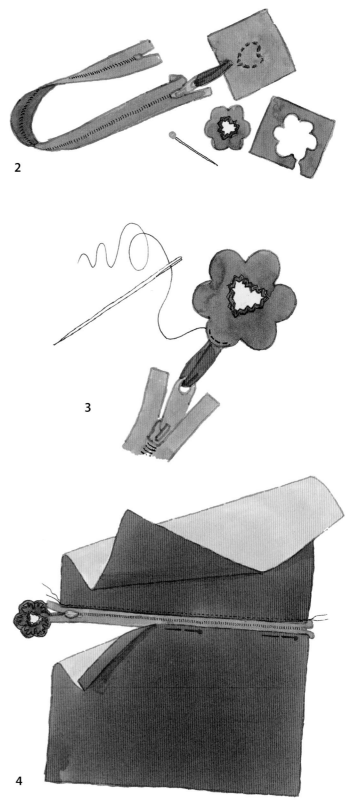

2

3

4

Attach the other piece of lining onto the other side of zip in the same way (**see picture 4**).

Press the lining away from the zip teeth.

JOINING THE OUTER BAG TO THE ZIP Turn the zip right side up, so the lining is wrong side up and spread out flat. Align the top edge of the back of the make-up bag as close as possible to the teeth on one side of the zip, with the wrong side of the bag to the right side of the zip, and the daisy zip pull on the left. Pin and tack in place. Using the zipper foot on your sewing machine, machine stitch in place, sewing close to the teeth of the zip and starting and finishing 1cm (½in) in from the sides of the make-up bag. Take care to ensure that the stitching goes through both layers of the bag and lining. Machine stitch a second parallel row 1cm (½in) away from the first. Pin and then tack the top edge of the front of the make-up bag to the other side of the zip in the same way, with the daisy zip pull on the right (**see picture 5**). Secure with two rows of machine stitching as before.

SEWING UP THE BAG Bring the front and back of the lining and outer pieces together to form the make-up bag, and pin and tack through all four layers along the sides and bottom seams (**see picture 6**).

Using black thread, machine stitch along the two sides and bottom of the bag, sewing close to the edge. Machine stitch a second row parallel to the first, 1cm (½in) from the edge.

Press flat (see note on page 107) and trim the edges to neaten, as necessary.

EMBROIDERY Using all six strands of pink embroidery thread, edge both sides and the bottom of the make-up bag with blanket stitch. Work neat stitches using the inner machine-stitched line as a guide and spacing them 1cm (½in) apart.

Finishing

Lightly press the finished bag with a slightly damp cloth between the fabric and the iron to prevent it from becoming shiny.

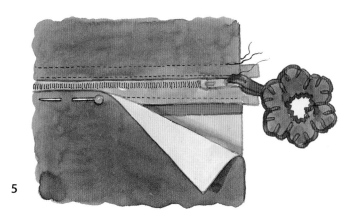

5

6

Vintage Rose Cushion

Taken from one of my best-selling collections, the Vintage Rose heart-shaped design, with its vibrant and luscious combination of deep pink and red roses with fresh green foliage, is an irresistible favourite. It is probably the most intricate appliqué design in the book and requires a certain amount of expertise to complete it.

Embroidery stitches

Blanket stitch appliqué (see page 140), chain stitch, zigzag chain stitch (see page 141), satin stitch (see pages 142–3), French knots (see page 142) and blanket stitch edging (see page 140), plus buttonhole stitch for the buttonholes (see page 141), or use the sewing machine.

Preparation

Prepare the wool fabric by pressing (see tips on page 105).

Using a photocopier, enlarge the front cushion pattern with the vintage rose heart design and the back cushion pattern by 250 per cent. At full size, the heart measures 30cm (12in) across at the widest point. Enlarge the different coloured appliqué design templates printed in reverse on page 127 by 200 per cent.

CUTTING OUT Referring to the notes on page 106, cut out one cushion front and two cushion backs in cream wool felt. Cut out two back facings in cream cotton and two in iron-on interfacing.

Appliqué

Using dressmaker's carbon paper between the right side of the fabric and the template (see page 106), trace the outline of the heart design and the areas to be appliquéd onto the centre of the front cushion piece (see picture 1).

The different coloured appliqué elements have been printed in reverse on page 127, to be enlarged on

1

Materials and equipment

45 x 45cm (18 x 18in) feather
  cushion pad
50cm (20in) of cream wool felt
  (minimum width 130cm/51in)
  for the cushion cover
25 x 25cm (9 x 9in) of red wool felt
  for the red roses
25 x 25cm (9 x 9in) of pink wool felt
  for the pink roses
25 x 25cm (9 x 9in) of green wool
  felt for the leaves
Two 4 x 46cm (1¾ x 18in) pieces of
  cream cotton fabric for the back
  opening facings
Three pieces of bonding web
  25 x 25cm (9 x 9in)
10 x 50cm (4 x 20in) of iron-on
  interfacing
Two buttons, 2cm (¾in) diameter
Cushion front pattern with vintage rose
  heart design template (page 126)
Appliqué templates (reversed) for
  roses and leaves (page 127)
Back cushion and facing patterns
  (page 129)
Sharp, hard pencil
Dressmaker's carbon paper
Masking tape
Embroidery kit and stranded cotton
  embroidery thread (dyefast) in
  light red, deep red, bright green,
  dark green, bright pink and yellow
Sewing machine, matching thread
  and sewing kit
Iron and ironing cloth

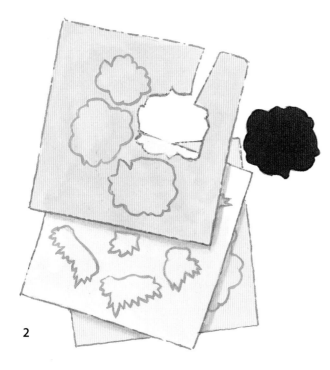

2

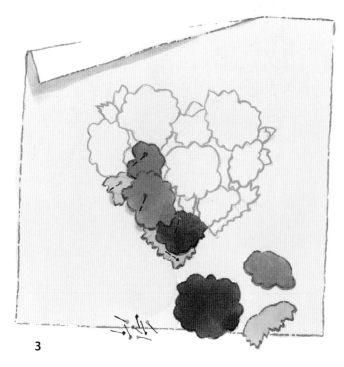

3

a photocopier and traced onto the bonding web, so that the shapes will be the right way around when they have been cut out. Following the bonding-web instructions for the Love Throw (see page 12), trace all the red roses onto one sheet of bonding web, trace all the pink roses onto another sheet and, finally, all the green leaves onto a third. Some of the pieces include areas of underlap (marked with slotted lines), which will fit under the adjacent motif on the heart design. This is to secure the appliqué shapes where the embroidery only holds down the edges.

Iron each piece of bonding web onto the wrong side of the corresponding pieces of red, pink and green wool felt, and then carefully cut out the roses and leaf shapes (see picture 2).

BUILDING UP THE DESIGN Peel off the bonding-web backing and position the roses and leaves as indicated on the front cushion piece, in sequence, right side up, to form the heart. Start with the leaves that appear from behind the roses, and pin them in the correct positions on the front cushion piece.

Refer to the photograph and template to see which elements overlap next, and pin them in place (see picture 3). Using an ironing cloth between the hot iron and the fabric to protect it, iron to fuse the shapes to the cushion front.

EMBROIDERY Using three strands of embroidery thread, outline the appliqué roses and leaves with zigzag chain stitch or satin stitch in the light red, bright pink and bright green threads, matching the elements you are stitching (see picture 4).

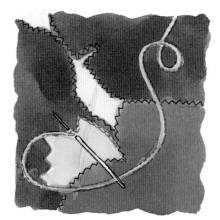

4

Use dressmaker's carbon paper to transfer the inner detail on the roses and leaves onto the design.

For the smaller leaves and stems, outline the shapes with chain stitch and infill with satin stitch using six strands of bright green embroidery thread. Do the same for the rosebuds using six strands of deep red embroidery thread **(see picture 5)**.

Work the inner detail on the roses and leaves in fine chain stitch using two strands each of the light red, bright pink and dark green embroidery threads.

Work the stamens in fine chain stitch using two strands of yellow embroidery thread and finish with French knots using three strands of yellow thread **(see picture 6)**.

Making up the cushion

Refer to the instructions and illustrations 4–7 for the oblong Lips Cushion on pages 18–19.

BACK FACINGS Using the iron, press iron-on interfacing to the wrong side of the cotton back facings. Turn one long edge of each facing under by 1cm (½in) and press the hem in place (see picture 4, page 18).

With right sides together, pin and tack the other long edge of each facing to one of the wool felt cushion back pieces, then machine stitch the 1cm (½in) seams (see picture 5, page 18).

Press the seams open and then fold the facings back onto the wrong side of the cushion backs and press. Pin, tack and machine a line of stitching 3.5cm (1½in) from the edge to hold the facing in place. Machine two parallel lines of stitching, one along each edge and the other 1cm (½in) in from the edge (see picture 6, page 19).

BUTTONHOLES Mark two buttonhole positions on the wrong side of the upper cushion back piece, positioning them 2cm (¾in) above the edge and 12cm (4¾in) apart. Work two 2.5cm (1in) buttonholes by machine or by hand.

5

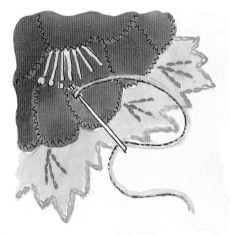

6

EMBROIDERY On the upper back piece, work blanket stitch along the edge of the opening with six strands of bright pink thread, using the inner machine-stitched line as a guide and spacing the stitches 1cm (½in) apart (see picture 7, page 19).

JOINING THE FRONT AND BACK Lay the upper back piece over the lower back piece, matching up the seams at the sides. Sew two buttons onto the lower cushion back at the marked points, corresponding with the buttonholes on the upper back piece **(see picture 7)**. Do up the buttons and tack the two pieces of the cushion back together to secure.

With wrong sides together, pin the front and back of the cushion together, then tack and machine stitch 1cm (½in) seams around all four edges. Machine a parallel stitch line along the outer edge of the cushion **(see picture 8)**.

EMBROIDERY Remove the tacking, press flat and trim the edges of the fabric if necessary to neaten.

Using all six strands of bright pink embroidery thread, edge the cushion with blanket stitch. Work neat stitches using the inner machine-stitched line as a guide and spacing them 1cm (½in) apart (see picture 9, page 19).

Finishing

Lightly press the finished cushion cover with a slightly damp cloth between the hot iron and the fabric to prevent it from becoming shiny.

Insert the cushion pad and do up the buttons.

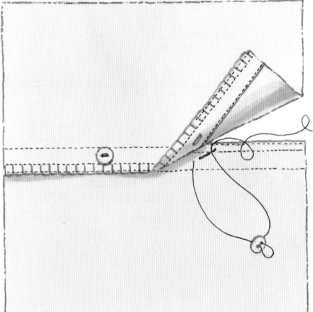

7

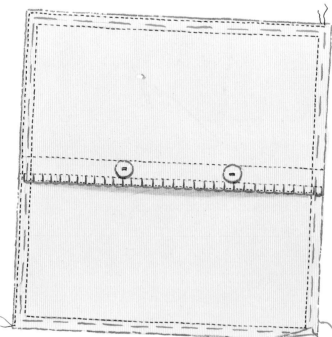

8

Flying the Flag

Five-Star Apron

The perfect accessory for five-star chefs, this traditional blue gingham apron with a convenient front pocket features a configuration of five striking, red appliqué stars on the bodice. A lovely present for the cook of the household, this apron could also be stitched using a heart motif instead of the stars, or even large initials.

Embroidery stitches

Blanket stitch appliqué (see page 140).

Preparation

Wash the gingham and red cotton fabrics and iron them while still damp to reduce shrinkage (see tips on page 105).

Using a photocopier, enlarge the apron pattern by 400 per cent. The star template is shown on page 125 at full size.

CUTTING OUT Referring to the notes on page 106, cut out the apron and the facing in blue gingham.

Then cut out two waist ties measuring 100 x 9cm (39½ x 3½in), one neckband measuring 58 x 9cm (23 x 3½in), and one pocket measuring 41.5 x 22cm (18 x 8¾in) in the blue gingham.

Appliqué

Following the bonding-web instructions for the Love Throw (see page 12), trace five star motifs onto the bonding web using a sharp pencil.

Iron the bonding web onto the wrong side of the red cotton and carefully cut out the stars on the inside of the pencil line.

Peel off the bonding-web backing and pin the stars, right sides up, in position on the front bodice of the apron, as indicated on the pattern. Iron to fuse the stars in place (**see picture 1**).

EMBROIDERY Using four strands of cream embroidery thread, outline the stars with blanket stitch, making small stitches about 5mm (¼in) long and spacing them 5mm (¼in) apart.

When the embroidery is complete, press carefully with a medium-hot iron (see note on page 107).

Materials and equipment

1m (1yd) of mid-blue cotton gingham (minimum width 110cm/43in) for the apron

25 x 25cm (9 x 9in) of red cotton fabric (dyefast) for the stars

25 x 25cm (9 x 9in) of bonding web

Apron pattern (page 125)

Stars motif template (page 125)

Sharp, hard pencil

Embroidery kit and stranded cotton embroidery thread (dyefast) in cream

Sewing machine, matching thread and sewing kit

Iron

1

Making up the apron

POCKET Start by hemming the top edge of the pocket. To do this, first fold the top edge 5mm (¼in) to the wrong side and pin and press. Then turn over another 1cm (½in) and pin, tack and machine stitch two rows, one along the edge and the other 8mm (³⁄₈in) in from the edge.

Fold the other three edges of the pocket 1cm (½in) to the wrong side and pin, tack and press.

Position the pocket on the front of the apron, as indicated on the pattern, and pin and tack it in place along the sides and bottom. Then machine stitch two rows, one along the edge and the other 8mm (³⁄₈in) in from the edge. Reinforce the top corners by machine stitching a diagonal line from the outer corner to the point where the inner stitch lines meet. Then machine stitch a vertical line through the centre of the pocket, from the top edge to the bottom, to divide it in half. Remove all the tacking thread once the machine stitching is complete (**see picture 2**).

NECKBAND Make up the neckband by folding the strip of fabric in half lengthways with right sides together. Pin, tack and machine stitch a 1cm (½in) seam down the long edge, leaving both ends open (**see picture 3**). Turn the fabric through to the right side, press the neckband flat and topstitch along both edges.

WAIST TIES Make up the two waist ties by folding the strips of fabric in half lengthways with right sides together. Pin, tack and machine stitch a 1cm (½in) seam down the long edge, sewing diagonally across one end 4cm (1½in) from the bottom and leaving the other end open. Trim off the corners at the pointed end and turn the fabric through to the right side. Press the waist tie flat and neatly turn in 1cm (½in) at the open end. Repeat for the other tie and topstitch all around the edge of both ties (**see picture 4**).

NECK FACING Hem the bottom edge of the neck facing in the same way as the top edge of the pocket, first turning over 5mm (¼in) and then turning over another 1cm (½in). As before, machine stitch two rows, one along the edge and the other 8mm (³⁄₈in) in from the edge.

Before attaching the facing to the inside of the apron bodice, position one end of the neckband on each side of the neckline as indicated on the pattern, with right sides together. Pin, tack and machine stitch in place.

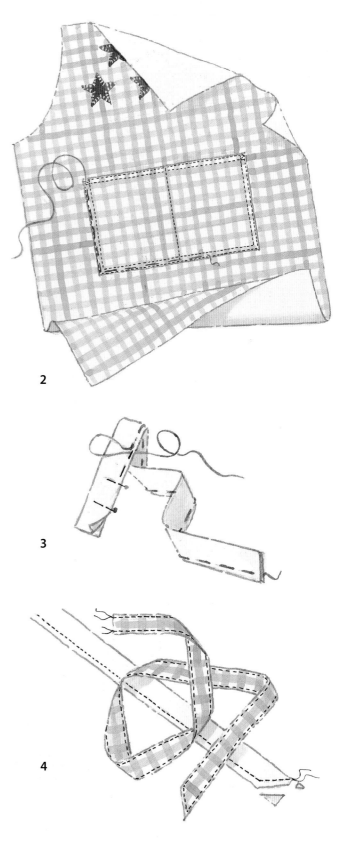

2

3

4

With right sides together (and the neckband in between), pin, tack and machine stitch the facing to the neckline of the apron with a 1cm (½in) seam allowance (see picture 5).

Turn the apron and facing right sides out and press. Topstitch along the edge of the neckline and then stitch another row parallel to it, 8mm (³⁄₈in) apart.

HEMMING THE APRON Hem the sides and bottom of the apron as described above. You will need to snip into the seam allowance at intervals around the curved bodice, so that the seam lies flat. As before, first fold 5mm (¼in) to the wrong side and then fold over another 1cm (½in). Machine stitch two parallel rows, one close to the edge and the other 8mm (³⁄₈in) in from the first.

ATTACHING THE WAIST TIES With the apron wrong side up, position the square end of one waist tie on each side of the apron, as marked on the pattern. Make sure the end of each tie overlaps the edge of the apron by 2.5cm (1in), and pin and then tack them in place. Attach the ties securely by machine stitching a square over the end of each tie and then sewing diagonally from corner to corner in both directions to form a cross (see picture 6).

Finishing

Press the finished apron on the reverse side (see notes on pressing and finishing on page 107).

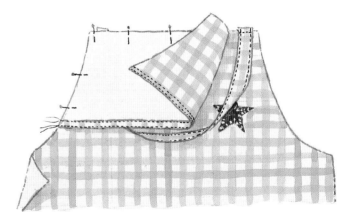

5

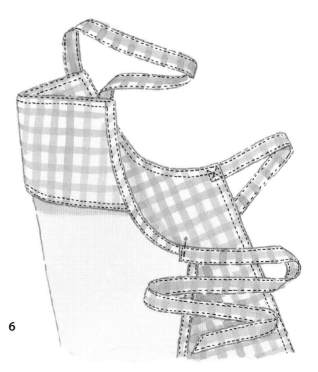

6

Union Flag Cushion

Since I first stitched this design more than five years ago, it has been my bestselling cushion. New-found patriotism, along with a resurgence in popularity of craft and all things vintage, has inspired the British nation to fly the flag again. The Union Flag is now as popular a decorative element as it was in the 1960s, when it was elevated to iconic status in the design world. Once you have mastered the basic technique shown here, it is not too difficult to adapt the design to make flag cushions for other nations.

Embroidery stitches

Cross stitch (see page 142), blanket stitch appliqué and blanket stitch edging (see page140), plus buttonhole stitch for the buttonholes (see page 141), or use the sewing machine.

Preparation

Prepare the wool fabric by pressing (see tips on page 105).

Using a photocopier, enlarge the front cushion pattern with the heart, cross and diagonal band templates and the back cushion and facing patterns by 220 per cent.

CUTTING OUT Referring to the notes on page 106, cut out one cushion front and two cushion backs in grey wool felt. Cut out two back facings in grey cotton and two in iron-on interfacing.

Then cut out the two wide cross bands, measuring 47.5 x 7cm (18¾ x 2¾in) and 36 x 7cm (14⅛ x 2¾in), in cream wool felt. Cut out the two wide diagonal bands (to pair), each measuring 59.5 x 4cm (23½ x 1½in), in cream wool felt. Trim the corners to fit.

Appliqué

Following the bonding-web instructions for the Love Throw (see page 12), trace the heart design, the two narrow cross bands and the two narrow diagonal bands onto the bonding web using a sharp pencil.

Iron the bonding web onto the wrong side of the red wool felt and carefully cut out the heart shape and the bands inside the pencil lines.

Materials and equipment

34 x 50cm (13½ x 20in) feather cushion pad

50cm (20in) of grey wool felt (minimum width 130cm/51in) for the cushion cover

15cm (6in) of cream wool felt (minimum width 110cm/43in) for the wide cross and diagonal bands

15cm (6in) of red wool felt (minimum width 70cm/28in) for the narrow cross and diagonal bands and the red heart

Two 4 x 36cm (1¾ x 14in) pieces of grey cotton fabric (dyefast) for the back opening facings

40 x 40cm (16 x 16in) of bonding web

10 x 40cm (4 x 16in) of iron-on interfacing

Two buttons, 2cm (¾in) diameter

Front cushion pattern with heart, cross and diagonal band design templates (page 114)

Back cushion and facing patterns (page 115)

Sharp, hard pencil

Tailor's chalk or marking pencil

Metal ruler

Embroidery kit and stranded cotton embroidery thread (dyefast) in red and cream

Sewing machine, matching thread, sewing kit and thimble

Iron and ironing cloth

1

MAKING UP THE BANDS Peel off the bonding-web backing and position each red band lengthways onto the centre of the corresponding cream band. Using an ironing cloth between the hot iron and the wool felt to protect it, iron to fuse the strips together (**see picture 1**).

Working on the narrow diagonal bands first, machine stitch close to the edges of the red band. Set the machine to a large stitch length (three stitches to 1cm/½in) and topstitch two parallel rows between the stitched edges (approximately 3mm/⅛in apart), so that the spacing is equal between the four rows. Repeat this with the wider cross bands, spacing the two lines of topstitching equally apart (approximately 12mm/½in) between the stitched edges (**see picture 2**).

ATTACHING THE BANDS Using a ruler and tailor's chalk or a marking pencil, mark the positions of the cross and diagonal bands onto the front cushion piece. Matching the corners and using the guidelines, lay one diagonal band in place. Pin, tack and machine stitch the band close to the cream edge on both sides. Lay the second diagonal band in place and repeat the above (**see picture 3**).

Lay the horizontal cross strip in place, using the chalk guidelines. Pin, tack and machine stitch the band close to the cream edge on both sides. Repeat for the vertical cross strip.

2

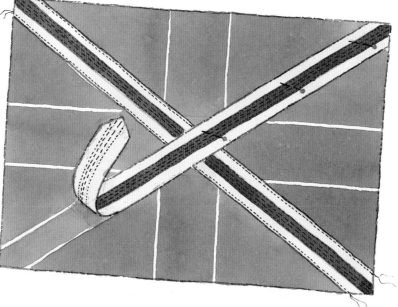

3

4

5

ATTACHING THE HEART Pin and then tack the heart onto the centre of the Union Flag cushion front, right side up **(see picture 4)**. Using an ironing cloth as before, iron to fuse it in place.

EMBROIDERY Using four strands of red embroidery thread, cross stitch evenly along the grey base wool felt and the cream edges of the diagonal and cross strips. Make the stitches 1cm (½in) long and 5mm (¼in) wide.

Using four strands of cream embroidery thread, carefully outline the heart with blanket stitch, making the stitches 5mm (¼in) long and spacing them 5mm (¼in) apart. The layers of appliqué will be quite thick in some areas, so it is advisable to use a thimble for protection **(see picture 5)**.

Making up the cushion

Make up the Union Flag Cushion in the same way as the Lips Cushion (see pages 18–19), but use six strands of cream rather than red embroidery thread for the blanket stitching on the edge of the back opening and around the edges of the finished cushion cover.

Finishing

Lightly press the finished cushion cover with a slightly damp cloth between the hot iron and the fabric to prevent it from becoming shiny.

Insert the cushion pad and do up the buttons.

Flag Placemats

These simple but very decorative placemats, stitched in the Swedish flag design, inject a vibrant dash of colour and patriotism into this cool and calm table setting. The design could be customized using the flag of any nation on the front of the placemat, with the lining and interlining stitched as described here. It would be fun to represent several nations with an array of different flag placemats at a dinner table. For instance, the templates for the front of the Union Flag Cushion or the flap of the Tricolour Bag could easily be adapted to make placemats, while this Swedish flag design could be made into a cushion or a bag.

Embroidery stitches

Blanket stitch edging (see page 140) and cross stitch (see page 142).

Preparation

Wash the linen, and iron while still damp to prevent shrinkage (see tips on page 105).

CUTTING OUT Referring to the notes on cutting out on page 106, cut out one placemat front in blue linen, one placemat lining in blue cotton and one in heat-resistant interlining, all measuring 47.5 x 32.5cm (18¾ x 12¾in).

Cut out one horizontal and one vertical strip in yellow linen, measuring 47.5 x 8.5cm (18¾ x 3½in) and 32.5 x 8.5cm (12¾ x 3½in), respectively.

Appliqué

Referring to the placemat diagram on page 135 and using a ruler and tailor's chalk, mark the positions of the horizontal and vertical bands on the front of the blue linen placemat front.

ATTACHING THE BANDS Fold each long side of the yellow bands 1cm (½in) to the wrong side, and press in place.

Using the chalk lines as a guide, place the horizontal band, right side up, onto the front of the placemat, and pin and tack in place **(see picture 1)**.

Materials and equipment

The fabric quantities given below are for one placemat, so please increase according to the number of placemats required.

50 x 30cm (20 x 12in) of blue linen (dyefast) for the placemat front

50 x 30cm (20 x 12in) of blue cotton (dyefast) for the placemat lining

50 x 20cm (20 x 8in) of yellow linen (dyefast) for the cross detail

50 x 30cm (20 x 12in) of heat-resistant interlining

Placemat diagram (page 135)

Metal ruler

Tailor's chalk or marking pencil

Embroidery kit and stranded cotton embroidery thread (dyefast) in yellow

Sewing machine, matching thread and sewing kit

Iron

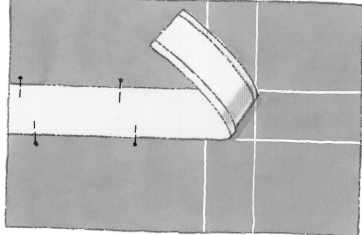

1

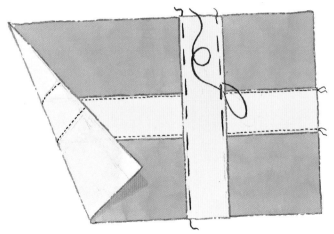

2

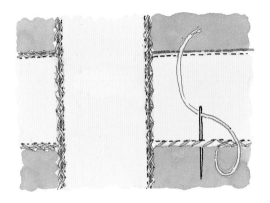

3

Machine stitch along both long edges of the horizontal band using matching yellow thread.

Repeat with the vertical strip, placing it over the top of the long horizontal strip, again following the chalk lines as a guide **(see picture 2)**.

EMBROIDERY Using all six strands of yellow embroidery thread, work neat cross stitch along both sides of the vertical band, making the stitches approximately 1cm (½in) long and 5mm (¼in) apart.

Work cross stitch along both sides of the horizontal band, up to the crossover of the vertical band on both sides **(see picture 3)**.

Making up the placemat

Pin and then tack the heat-resistant interlining onto the blue cotton placemat lining with wrong sides together.

With right sides together, pin and tack the front of the placemat to the lining **(see picture 4)**.

Machine stitch around the rectangle with a 1cm (½in) seam allowance, leaving a 10cm (4in) gap in the seam on the bottom edge. Clip the corners to reduce the bulk, remove the tacking and turn the placemat through to the right side **(see picture 5)**.

Pull out the corners and press carefully around the edges, folding in and pressing the 1cm (½in) seam allowance at the open area along the bottom edge. Machine stitch all around the edge of the placemat, sewing one row close to the edge and a second row parallel to the first, 1cm (½in) in.

EMBROIDERY Using six strands of yellow embroidery thread, work blanket stitch around the edge of the placemat, using the machine-stitched lines as a guide and making the stitches 1cm (½in) long and spacing them 1cm (½in) apart **(see picture 6)**.

Finishing

Press carefully to finish (see note on pressing and finishing on page 107).

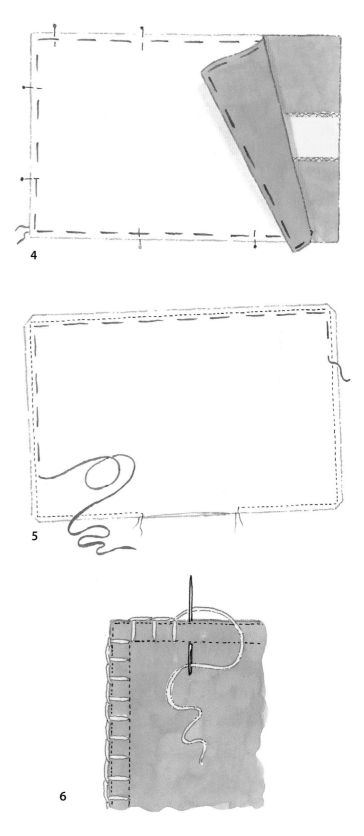

4

5

6

Stars & Stripes Heart Cushion

Why not put one of your favourite flags inside a heart and stitch it with love, or adapt this cushion for a friend overseas to remind them of home? The design is appliquéd onto a heart-shaped base and stitched onto the back of the cushion front with a cut-out heart. Symbolic and strong, the bold stripes and dreamy stars are a perfect combination.

Embroidery stitches

Blanket stitch appliqué (see page 140), cross stitch (see page 142) and blanket stitch edging (see page 140), plus buttonhole stitch for the buttonholes (see page 141), or use the sewing machine.

Preparation

Prepare the wool fabric by pressing (see tips on page 105).

Using a photocopier, enlarge the front cushion pattern with the heart, stars and stripes design template and the back cushion and facing patterns by 250 per cent.

CUTTING OUT Referring to the notes on cutting out on page 106, cut out one cushion front and two cushion backs in cream wool felt.

Cut out two back facings in cotton and two in iron-on interfacing.

Transfer the outline of the cut-out heart onto the cushion front piece using dressmaker's carbon paper between the fabric and the template (see page 106). Using a sharp pencil, trace around the smaller, inner heart to transfer it onto the centre of the cushion front on the wrong side of the wool felt. Carefully cut away the heart shape using sharp scissors (see picture 1).

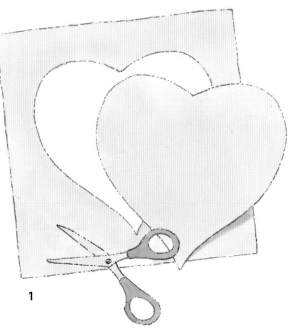

1

Materials and equipment

- 45 x 45cm (18 x 18in) feather cushion pad
- 70cm (28in) of cream wool felt (minimum width 130cm/51in) for the cushion cover and the reverse appliqué heart
- 25 x 25cm (9 x 9in) of red wool felt for the stripes
- 25 x 25cm (9 x 9in) of grey wool felt for the stars
- Two 4 x 46cm (1¾ x 17¾in) pieces of cream cotton fabric for the back opening facings
- Two 25 x 25cm (9 x 9in) pieces of bonding web
- 10 x 50cm (4 x 20in) of iron-on interfacing
- Two buttons, 2cm (¾in) diameter
- Front cushion pattern with heart, stars and stripes design template (page 128)
- Back cushion pattern (page 129)
- Dressmaker's carbon paper
- Masking tape
- Sharp, hard pencil
- Tailor's chalk or marking pencil
- Metal ruler
- Embroidery kit and stranded cotton embroidery thread (dyefast) in cream and red
- Sewing machine, matching thread and sewing kit
- Iron and ironing cloth

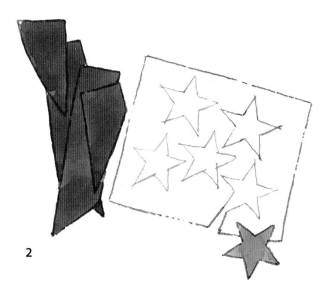

2

3

Appliqué

Using the outline for the larger, outer heart on the template, cut out the appliqué heart in cream wool felt to form the base for the embroidered design. Mark the stars and stripes onto it with tailor's chalk or a marking pencil, or transfer it using dressmaker's carbon paper, as before.

Following the bonding-web instructions for the Love Throw (see page 12) and using a sharp pencil, trace the four stripes onto one piece of bonding web and the five stars onto the other.

Iron the bonding web with the stripes marked on it onto the wrong side of the red wool felt and cut out the stripes. Iron the bonding web with the stars marked on it onto the wrong side of the grey wool felt and carefully cut out the stars **(see picture 2)**.

MAKING UP THE DESIGN Peel off the bonding-web backing and pin the stripes vertically onto the lower part of the heart shape, as indicated on the pattern, right sides up **(see picture 3)**. Using an ironing cloth between the hot iron and the fabric to protect it, iron to fuse the stripes to the heart-shaped base. Repeat this process to attach the stars onto the upper part of the heart.

EMBROIDERY Using four strands of cream embroidery thread, outline the stars with blanket stitch, sewing small stitches about 5mm (¼in) long and spacing them 5mm (¼in) apart.

Using four strands of red embroidery thread, work cross stitch, 5mm (¼in) long and 5mm (¼in) wide, along both edges of the stripes and horizontally across the top of the stripes. If you find

4

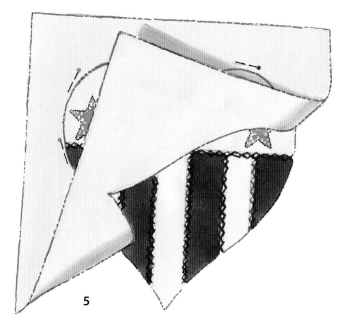

5

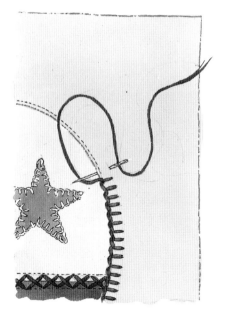

6

it easier, machine stitch two parallel lines 5mm (¼in) apart along the top of the stripes to use as a guide for your stitching **(see picture 4)**.

ATTACHING THE HEART With right sides facing up, position the larger appliqué stars and stripes heart under the cushion front and pin and then tack it in place, being careful not to stretch the shape of the smaller, cut-out heart **(see picture 5)**. Machine stitch the heart in place with a 5mm (¼in) seam.

EMBROIDERY Using six strands of red embroidery thread, work blanket stitch all around the heart, using the 5mm (¼in) seam as a guide and spacing the stitches 5mm (¼in) apart **(see picture 6)**.

Making up the cushion

Make up the Stars & Stripes Heart Cushion in the same way as the Vintage Rose Cushion (see pages 57–8), but use six strands of red embroidery thread, rather than pink, for the blanket stitching on the edge of the back opening and along the edges of the finished cushion cover.

Finishing

Lightly press the finished cushion cover with a slightly damp cloth between the hot iron and the fabric to prevent it from becoming shiny (see note on page 107).

Insert the cushion pad and do up the buttons.

Tricolour Flag Bag

Fly the flag on your shoulder when you carry your books or laptop inside this bag. The tricolour flag has been used in wonderful colour combinations by many different countries. The bag could be made in cotton canvas for a more masculine and robust version. *C'est très chic.*

Embroidery stitches

Blanket stitch edging (see page 140) and cross stitch (see page 142).

Preparation

Prepare the wool fabric by pressing (see tips on page 105).

Using a photocopier, enlarge the bag and lining patterns by 250 per cent.

CUTTING OUT Referring to the notes on cutting out on page 106, cut out one front bag piece, one back bag piece, one gusset, one left-hand strip for the front flap and one inside pocket in blue wool felt. Cut out one right-hand strip for the front flap in red wool felt.

For the lining, cut out one bag front, one bag back, one flap and one gusset in red cotton fabric.

Cut out one strip of blue wool felt for the shoulder strap measuring 110 x 10cm (43 x 4in), or shorter if required, using a ruler and tailor's chalk across the width of the fabric.

Cut out one central strip in cream wool felt for the front panel measuring 33 x 13cm (13 x 5in).

Making up the bag

FRONT FLAP Join the three front flap sections together with the blue strip on the left, the cream strip in the centre and the red strip on the right. To do this, pin and tack the long straight edges of the blue and red strips to each side of the central cream strip with right sides together. Machine stitch with 1cm (½in) seams, then press the seams open.

EMBROIDERY Using all six strands of red embroidery thread, work cross stitch along both seams, making the stitches 1cm (½in) long and 7mm (¼in) wide and keeping the seam in the centre of the stitches (**see picture 1**).

Materials and equipment

- 50cm (20in) of blue wool felt for the bag (minimum width 130cm/51in)
- 35 x 20cm (14 x 8in) of red wool felt for the right-hand strip
- 35 x 20cm (14 x 8in) of cream wool felt for the central strip
- 35cm (14in) of red cotton fabric (dyefast) for the lining (minimum width 120cm/48in)
- Bag and lining patterns (pages 130–1)
- Metal ruler
- Tailor's chalk or marking pencil
- Embroidery kit and stranded cotton embroidery thread (dyefast) in cream and red
- Sewing machine, matching thread and sewing kit
- Iron and ironing cloth

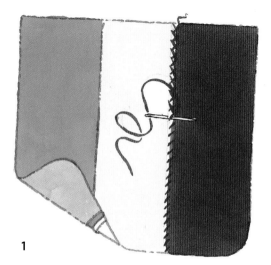

1

With right sides facing, pin and tack the tricolour flap and lining together. Machine stitch a 1cm (½in) seam along the three sides with curved corners to form the flap. Trim away the excess fabric at the corners and turn the flap through to the right side. Press the seamed edges carefully and machine stitch, in matching blue thread, close to the edge around the three sides of the flap. Machine stitch a second parallel row 1cm (½in) in from the edge.

POCKET To make the inside pocket, fold the facing to the wrong side along the fold line and pin, tack and machine stitch close to the edge. Pin and tack the pocket in position on the right side of the back lining, matching the balance points. Machine stitch along the two sides and the bottom of the pocket, close to the edge, and then stitch a second parallel row 1cm (½in) in from the edge. Machine stitch down the centre of the pocket to divide it in half, as marked on the pattern (**see picture 2**).

BAG FRONT With right sides facing, pin and tack the top edges of the front bag and front lining pieces together. Machine stitch a 1cm (½in) seam along the top edge, turn through to the right side and press the seam. Using matching blue thread, machine stitch along the edge, close to the seam, then stitch a second parallel row 1cm (½in) in from the edge.

With wrong sides facing, pin and tack the front bag and front lining together along the sides and bottom edge (**see picture 3**).

ATTACHING THE FLAP Join the front flap to the back bag and back lining pieces. To do this, first lay the back lining piece right side up on your work surface. Then lay the tricolour flap right side up on top of it – the flap will be 1cm (½in) narrower at each side to allow for the gusset seam, so position it centrally on the lining piece. Finally, lay the back bag piece wrong side up on top, aligning its edges with the lining. Pin, tack and machine stitch all three pieces together along the top edge with a 1cm (½in) seam (**see picture 4**).

Bring the back bag and back lining pieces wrong sides together and press them away from the tricolour flap. Thread the sewing machine with blue thread (to match the outer bag) and fill the bobbin with red thread (to match the lining). Machine stitch close to the edge of the seam on the back of the bag, then stitch a second parallel row 1cm (½in) away from the seam.

With wrong sides facing, pin and tack the back bag and back lining together along the sides and bottom edge.

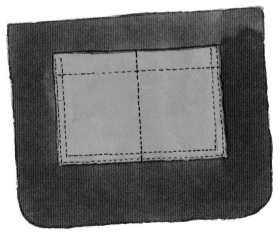

2

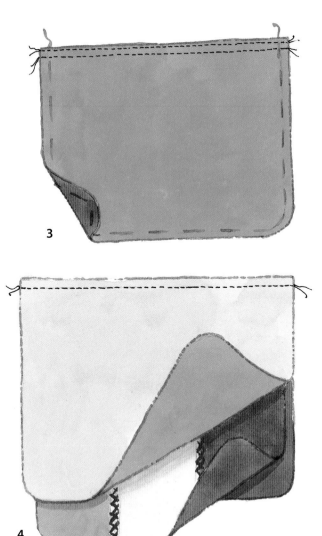

3

4

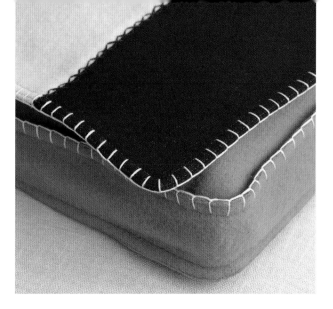

SHOULDER STRAP Make up the shoulder strap by folding the strip of blue wool felt in half lengthways with right sides together. Pin, tack and machine stitch a 1cm (½in) seam down the long edge, leaving both ends open. Gently press the seam open, turn through to the right side and press the strap flat with the seam in the centre. Machine stitch along both long edges of the strap and then stitch a second parallel row 1cm (½in) in from the edge on both sides.

Sandwich each end of the shoulder strap in between the narrow ends of the wool felt gusset and gusset lining. To do this, place the right sides of the strap and wool felt gusset together and the right side of the gusset lining to the wrong side of the strap, positioning the strap centrally. Pin, tack and machine stitch a 1cm (½in) seam **(see picture 5)**. Bring the gusset and gusset lining wrong sides together and press them away from the strap on both sides. Machine stitch across the gusset close to the seam, then stitch a second parallel row across the gusset 1cm (½in) away from the seam. Pin and tack the gusset and gusset lining together along both edges, with wrong sides together.

ATTACHING THE GUSSET With the right sides of the lining together, pin and tack the gusset to the front and back of the bag, matching the balance points. Machine stitch along the sides and bottom of the bag with a 1cm (½in) seam **(see picture 6)**. Stitch another parallel row close to the edge on both sides of the gusset.

EMBROIDERY Using all six strands of cream embroidery thread, work blanket stitch around three sides of the bag flap using the machine-stitched lines as a guide and making the stitches 1cm (½in) long and spacing them 1cm (½in) apart. Work blanket stitch in cream around the front edges/gusset seams of the bag. For durability, work blanket stitch on the back edges/gusset as well.

Finishing

Lightly press the finished bag (see note on page 107).

Alternative tricolour flag

To represent the Italian tricolour flag, for instance, instead of the French flag, simply use green wool felt instead of blue (see right). You could also adapt the front flap pattern to make a horizontal tricolour flag, such as the Estonian flag which has a blue stripe above, a black stripe in the centre and a white stripe below.

5

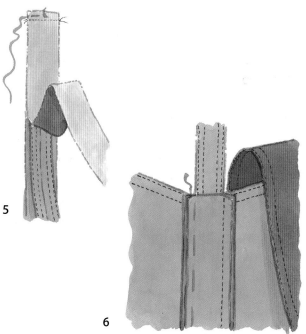

6

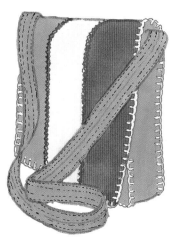

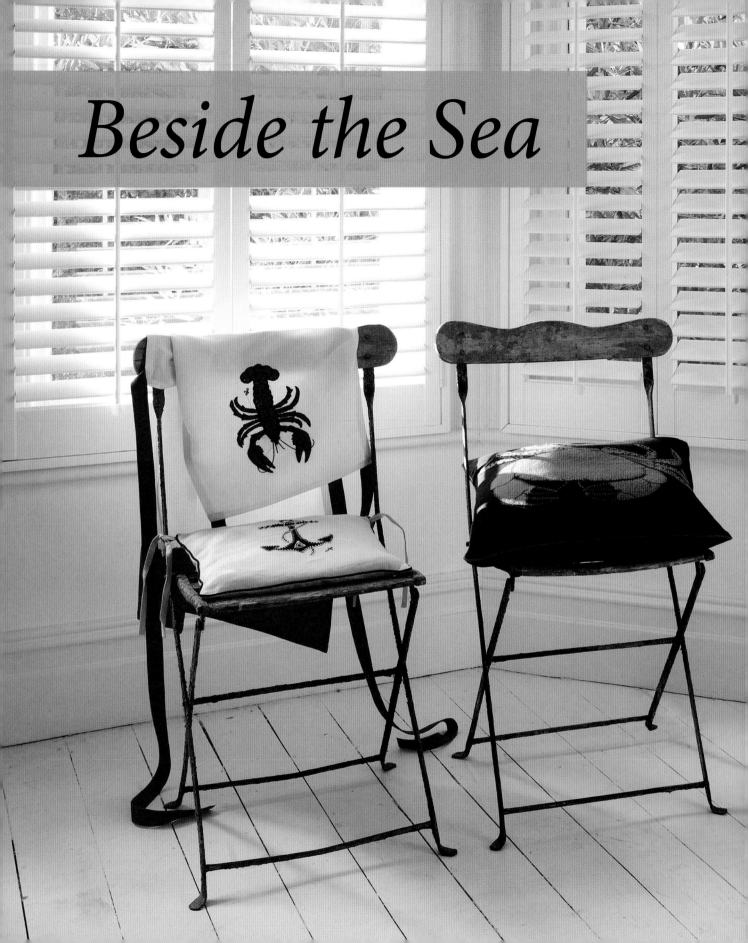

Beside the Sea

Crab Cushion

I was inspired to design this crab cushion while holidaying at Port Isaac in Cornwall, where crabs are in abundance. They are found in the rock pools where the children play, in the daily catch by the village fishermen and on the menus of all the local restaurants. The design introduces a bright splash of colour and is perfect in a seaside home or kitchen.

Embroidery stitches

Blanket stitch appliqué (see page 140), zigzag chain stitch (see page 141) and French knots (see page 142), plus buttonhole stitch for the buttonholes (see page 141), or use the sewing machine.

Preparation

Wash and iron the linen and press the wool felt (see tips on page 105).

Using a photocopier, enlarge the front cushion pattern with the crab motif template and the back cushion pattern by 270 per cent.

TRACING THE DESIGN When the design is not symmetrical, as here, it needs to be traced in reverse before being traced through the bonding web, or the motif will appear the other way around on the finished cushion. Using a sharp pencil and tracing paper, trace the full-size crab motif in reverse onto a sheet of paper.

CUTTING OUT Referring to the notes on page 106, cut out one cushion front and two cushion backs in linen. Cut out two pieces of iron-on interfacings measuring 48 x 3cm (18¾ x 1⅛in).

PIPING For the piping, cut out a total of 2m (2yds) of bias-grain strips of contrasting orange dyefast cotton. To do this, fold the 50cm (20in) square of fabric diagonally so that one corner meets the other to form a triangle. Cut along the fold line. Using tailor's chalk, mark a parallel line 3cm (1¼in) from the cut edge and cut along this line to create a strip of fabric 3cm (1¼in) wide. Repeat to cut out four more strips to make a total of 2m (2yds). Machine stitch the four strips together, end to end, with 1cm (½in) seams, to make one strip long enough to go all the way around the edge of the cushion (**see picture 1**).

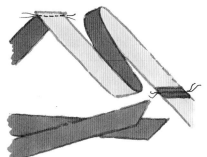

1

Materials and equipment

45 x 45cm (18 x 18in) cushion pad

70cm (28in) of natural linen (minimum width 110cm/43in wide) for the cushion cover

50 x 50cm (20 x 20in) of orange cotton fabric (dyefast) for the insertion piping

2m (2yds) of cotton piping cord, 3mm (⅛in) thick

40 x 40cm (16 x 16in) of orange wool felt for the crab

10 x 10cm (4 x 4in) of black wool felt for the pincers

40 x 40cm (16 x 16in) of bonding web for the crab

10 x 10cm (4 x 4in) of bonding web for the pincers

10 x 50cm (4 x 20in) of iron-on interfacing

Two buttons, 2cm (¾in) diameter

Front cushion pattern with crab motif template (page 132)

Back cushion pattern (page 133)

Tracing paper and sheet of paper

Sharp, hard pencil

Tailor's chalk or marking pencil

Metal ruler

Dressmaker's carbon paper

Masking tape

Embroidery kit and stranded cotton embroidery thread (dyefast) in black and orange

Sewing machine, matching thread and sewing kit

Iron and ironing cloth

Appliqué

Following the bonding-web instructions for the Love Throw (see page 12), trace the outline of the reversed crab motif (without the pincers) onto the bonding web using a sharp pencil. In the same way, trace the outline of the reversed pincers onto another piece of bonding web.

Iron the bonding web with the crab marked on it onto the wrong side of the orange wool felt and carefully cut it out inside the pencil lines **(see picture 2)**. Iron the bonding web with the pincers on it onto the wrong side of the black wool felt and cut them out.

Peel off the bonding-web backing and pin the crab and the pincers, right sides up, into position on the front piece of the cushion **(see picture 3)**. Using an ironing cloth between the hot iron and the wool felt to protect it, iron to fuse the pieces in place.

EMBROIDERY Using dressmaker's carbon paper between the fabric and the template (see page 106), trace over the inner details of the design to transfer them onto the crab shape.

Using four strands of black embroidery thread, outline the crab with blanket stitch, making small stitches about 5mm (¼in) long and spacing them 5mm (¼in) apart. Work on the main body of the crab first, then the legs.

Outline the pincers with blanket stitch in the same way, using four strands of orange embroidery thread.

For the inner detail, work zigzag chain stitch using two strands of black embroidery thread.

Work chain stitch for the antennae using three strands of orange embroidery thread.

Finish with French knots for the eyes, using six strands of black embroidery thread, and for the spots, using four strands of black embroidery thread **(see picture 4)**.

When the embroidery is complete, press from the back lightly, taking care not to flatten the French knots (see page 107).

Making up the cushion

PIPING To make the piping for the cushion edges, fold the bias strip of contrasting cotton in half over the piping cord and pin, tack and machine stitch close to the piping **(see picture 5)**.

With the embroidered side of the cushion front facing upwards and the piping cord facing inwards, pin the piping all around the

2

3

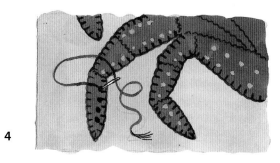

4

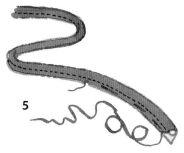

5

edge of the cushion front, aligning the raw edges and easing the piping around the corners, clipping into the seam allowance as necessary. When you reach the place where you started, cut the inner cord so that the ends butt together and firmly overstitch. Trim the piping fabric so that the ends overlap each other and turn one end under by 1cm (½in). Tuck the other raw end underneath it and stitch. Tack and then machine stitch the piping in place (see picture 6).

BACK FACINGS Using the iron, press iron-on interfacing onto the back of each facing section on the back cushion pieces. Fold the outer edge 1cm (½in) to the wrong side and press the hem in place. Fold back the facing sections at the balance points, so that wrong sides are together, press and then topstitch along the fold. Pin, tack and machine stitch the facings in place 2.5cm (1in) from the edge of the fold (see picture 7).

BUTTONHOLES Mark the buttonhole positions on the wrong side of the top back piece and work two 2cm (¾in) buttonholes by hand or by machine. Sew two buttons into position at the marked points on the lower back cushion piece.

With the centre back balance points matching at the sides, overlap the top back cushion piece with the bottom back cushion piece, and pin and tack in place.

JOINING THE FRONT AND BACK With right sides together, pin and tack the front and back cushion pieces together (see picture 8). Machine stitch around the edge of the cushion, following the previous stitch line made for the piping and pivoting the needle at the corners to allow for the bulk of the piping.

Trim the corners to reduce the bulk and neaten the raw edges. Turn the cushion cover through to the right side and pull the corners into shape.

Finishing

Lightly press the edges with the tip of the iron and press the finished cushion cover with a slightly damp cloth between the fabric and the iron to prevent it from becoming shiny.

Insert the cushion pad and do up the buttons.

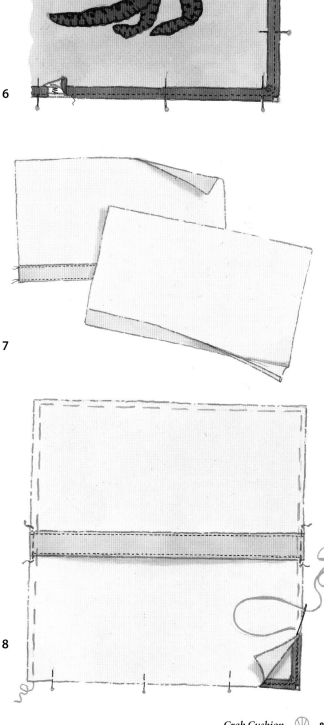

6

7

8

Anchor Seat Pad

This little linen seat pad, which ties onto the back of the chair, has been stitched with an appliqué anchor, my favourite maritime motif. It sits on a mahogany child's chair, but the pattern could be tailor-made to fit any chair. Alternatively, use the cutting pattern for the Crab Cushion.

Note: This seat pad, which measures 36 x 36cm (13¾ x 13¾in), can be adapted to fit a larger chair by tracing the outline of the seat or by measuring it and adding a 1cm (½in) seam allowance and 5cm (2in) back facings, as seen on the pattern on pages 136–7. Extra piping and padding will also be required.

Embroidery stitches
Blanket stitch appliqué (see page 140), chain stitch and zigzag chain stitch (see page 141).

Preparation
Wash and iron the linen (see tips on page 105).

Using a photocopier, enlarge the front seat-pad pattern with the anchor motif template and the back, facing and tie seat-pad patterns by 250 per cent.

TRACING THE DESIGN When the design is not symmetrical, as here, it needs to be traced in reverse before being traced through the bonding web, or the motif will appear the other way around on the finished seat pad. Using a sharp pencil and tracing paper, trace the full-size anchor motif in reverse onto a sheet of paper.

CUTTING OUT Referring to the notes on cutting out on page 106, cut out one seat-pad front, two seat-pad backs and four ties in the natural linen. Cut out two facings in iron-on interfacing.

PIPING For the piping, cut out a total of 1.5m (1¾yds) of bias-grain strips of black cotton or linen. To do this, fold the 50cm (20in) square of fabric diagonally so that one corner meets the other to form a triangle. Cut along the fold line. Using tailor's chalk, mark a parallel line 3cm (1¼in) from the cut edge and cut along this line to

Materials and equipment
60cm (23½in) of natural linen (minimum width 90cm/35½in) for the seat-pad cover

Piece of wadding/foam (cut to fit – approximately 36 x 36cm/13¾ x 13¾in)

50 x 5cm (20 x 2in) of black cotton or linen fabric (dyefast) for the insertion piping and anchor appliqué

1.5m (1¾yds) of cotton piping cord, 3mm (⅛in) thick

20 x 20cm (8 x 8in) piece of bonding web

10 x 40cm (4 x 16in) of iron-on interfacing

Front seat-pad pattern with anchor motif template (page 136)

Back seat-pad pattern (page 137)

Tracing paper and sheet of paper

Sharp, hard pencil

Metal ruler

Tailor's chalk or marking pencil

Dressmaker's carbon paper

Masking tape

Embroidery kit and stranded cotton embroidery thread (dyefast) in cream and black

Sewing machine, matching thread and sewing kit

Iron and ironing cloth

1

create a strip of fabric 3cm (1¼in) wide. Repeat to cut out three more strips to make a total of 1.5m (1¾yds). Machine stitch the strips together, end to end with 1cm (½in) seams, to make one strip long enough to go all the way around the edge of the seat pad (see picture 1 for the Crab Cushion on page 84).

Appliqué

Following the bonding-web instructions for the Love Throw (see page 12), trace the reversed anchor motif onto the bonding web using a sharp pencil **(see picture 1, page 88)**.

Iron the bonding web with the anchor marked on it onto the wrong side of the black fabric and carefully cut out the shape inside the pencil lines. Peel off the bonding-web backing and pin the anchor, right side up, into position on the seat-pad front **(see picture 2)**. Iron to fuse the fabrics in place.

EMBROIDERY Using dressmaker's carbon paper between the fabric and the template (see page 106), trace the inner details of the design onto the appliqué anchor.

Using four strands of cream embroidery thread, outline the anchor with blanket stitch, making small, neat stitches about 5mm (¼in) long and spacing them 5mm (¼in) apart.

Using two strands of black embroidery thread, work zigzag chain stitch to form the rope and anchor detail, but work chain stitch for the detail on the lower part of the anchor **(see picture 3)**.

When the embroidery is complete, gently press with an iron from the back (see page 107).

Making up the seat pad

PIPING To make the piping for the seat-pad edges, fold the bias strip of black fabric in half over the piping cord and pin, tack and machine stitch close to the piping (see picture 5 for the Crab Cushion on page 86).

Starting at the top edge of the seat pad, pin, tack and machine stitch the piping all around the edge of the front seat-pad piece, with the embroidered side facing up and the piping cord facing inwards. Align the raw edges and ease the piping around the corners, clipping into the seam allowance as necessary. When you reach the place where you started, cut the inner cord so that the ends butt together and firmly

2

3

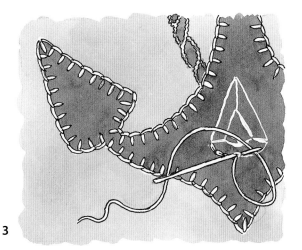

4

overstitch. Trim the piping fabric so that the ends overlap each other and turn one end under by 1cm (½in). Tuck the other raw end underneath it and stitch. Tack and then machine stitch the piping in place (see picture 6 for the Crab Cushion on page 87).

BACK FACINGS Using the iron, press iron-on interfacing onto the back of each facing section on the back seat-pad pieces. Fold the outer edge 1cm (½in) to the wrong side and press the hem in place, then machine stitch close to this edge. Fold back the facing sections at the balance points, so that wrong sides are together, and press **(see picture 4)**. Pin, tack and machine stitch the facings in place with a row of stitching 2.5cm (1in) from the edge.

With the centre back balance points matching at the sides, place the top back seat-pad piece so that it overlaps the bottom back seat-pad piece, and pin and tack in place **(see picture 5)**. Machine stitch at the sides to secure.

TIES Make up the four ties (two for each side) by folding the strips in half lengthways with right sides together. Pin, tack and machine stitch a 1cm (½in) seam down the length of each and across one end. Clip the corners diagonally to reduce bulk and turn the ties right side out using a safety pin to ease the fabric through. Press the ties flat and topstitch along the three edges **(see picture 6)**.

With the front seat-pad piece right side up, pin and tack two ties at right angles to each other in each corner, placing the open ends of the ties to the edge of the front seat-pad piece at the balance points, with the length of the ties towards the centre.

JOINING THE FRONT AND BACK With right sides together, pin and tack the front and back seat-pad pieces together, matching the balance points **(see picture 7)**. Machine stitch around the edge, following the previous stitch line made for the piping and pivoting the needle at the corners to allow for the piping's bulk.

Trim the corners to reduce the bulk and neaten the raw edges with scissors. Turn the seat-pad cover through to the right side and pull the corners into shape.

Finishing

Lightly press the edges with the tip of the iron and press the finished seat-pad cover with a slightly damp cloth between the fabric and the iron.

Insert the wadding/foam filling into the seat-pad cover.

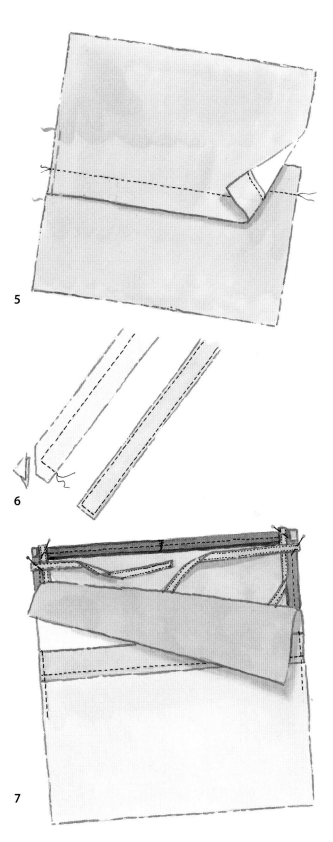

5

6

7

Galleon Wall Hanging

This wonderful design is based on the *Mayflower*, a galleon that sailed in 1620, taking the Pilgrims from Plymouth in England to Cape Cod in the USA to make a new life. Below the ship I have embroidered the first line of a favourite poem, 'A ship is a breath of romance...'

Embroidery stitches

Blanket stitch appliqué and blanket stitch edging (see page 140), chain stitch (see page 141), satin stitch (see pages 142–3) and French knots (see page 142).

Preparation

Prepare the cotton and wool felt fabrics by pressing (see tips on page 105).

Using a photocopier, enlarge the wall-hanging pattern with the galleon design template by 400 per cent.

TRACING THE DESIGN When the appliqué design is not symmetrical, as here, the elements need to be traced in reverse before being traced through the bonding web, so that they will appear the right way around on the finished design. Using a sharp pencil and tracing paper, trace the full-size hull, sails and flags in reverse onto a sheet of paper.

CUTTING OUT Referring to the notes on page 106, cut out one wall-hanging front piece in cream wool felt (72 x 72cm/28½ x 28½in). Cut out one wall-hanging lining in black cotton.

Cut out five hanging loops measuring 6 x 12cm (2½ x 4¾in) in cream wool felt. Cut out the strips required to make seven decorative tassels in cream wool felt and eight in black wool felt. For each tassel, cut one hanging loop measuring 1 x 6cm (½ x 2½in) and six strips measuring 1 x 26cm (½ x 10in).

Appliqué

Using dressmaker's carbon paper between the cream wool felt and the galleon design template (see page 106), trace the outline of the main appliqué shapes – the galleon's hull, sails and flags – into position on the right side of the wall-hanging front piece.

Materials and equipment

1m (1yd) of cream wool felt (minimum width 110cm/43in for the wall hanging, appliqué design, five hanging loops and seven tassels)

60 x 26cm (23½ x 10in) of black wool felt for eight tassels

10 x 10cm (4 x 4in) of grey wool felt for the flags

75cm (29½in) of black cotton fabric (dyefast, minimum width 110cm/43in) for the lining

Two pieces of bonding web, 60 x 45cm (23½ x 17¾in) and 10 x 10cm (4 x 4in)

15 wooden or plastic beads, approximately 1.5cm (¾in) diameter

Wall-hanging pattern with galleon design template (page 134)

Sharp, hard pencil

Tracing paper and sheet of paper

Dressmaker's carbon paper

Masking tape

25cm (9in) embroidery ring (optional)

Embroidery kit and stranded cotton embroidery thread (dyefast) in black, red and cream

Sewing machine, matching thread and sewing kit

Iron and ironing cloth

72cm (28½in) long (minimum) piece of wooden dowel, 1.5cm (¾in) diameter

1m (1yd) of red ribbon, 5mm (¼in) wide to hang

A ship is a breath of romance

Following the bonding-web instructions for the Love Throw (see page 12), trace the outline of the hull and sails (in reverse) onto the large piece of bonding web using a sharp pencil. Iron the bonding web onto the wrong side of a piece of cream felt. Trace the outline of the two flags (in reverse) onto the small piece of bonding web and iron it onto the piece of grey wool felt.

Cut out the hull, sails and flags, peel off the bonding-web backing and pin the appliqué shapes in position on the front of the wall hanging (see picture 1). Using an ironing cloth between the hot iron and the wool felt to protect it, iron to fuse the fabrics together.

EMBROIDERY As there is a lot of detail to embroider, it may be helpful to secure the fabric in an embroidery ring. Using four strands of black embroidery thread, work blanket stitch neatly around the outline of the hull, sails and flags, sewing small stitches 5mm (¼in) long and spacing them 5mm (¼in) apart.

Using dressmaker's carbon paper under the template, as before, trace the whole design onto the front of the wall hanging.

Using six strands of black embroidery thread, sew satin stitch for the masts and thicker black areas on the ship's hull.

Using six strands of red embroidery thread, sew satin stitch for the cross on the left flag.

Using four strands of red embroidery thread, sew satin stitch for the cross and diagonal bands on the right flag.

Using four strands of cream embroidery thread, work chain stitch for the outlines of the red crosses and diagonals on both flags.

For the rest of the details, follow the carbon-paper lines and work chain stitch with four strands of black embroidery thread. Where the rigging overlaps the black mast, sew chain stitch with four strands of cream embroidery thread instead of black.

Finish with the dots in the text, working them in French knots using four strands of black embroidery thread (see picture 2).

Making up the wall hanging

HANGING LOOPS Fold each of the five rectangles in half lengthways with right sides together and pin, tack and machine stitch a 1cm (½in) seam along the long edge. Press the seam open and turn the fabric right side out. Press the hanging loop flat with the seam in the centre. Machine stitch close to the edge along

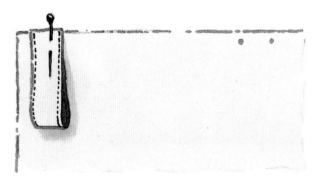

1

2

3

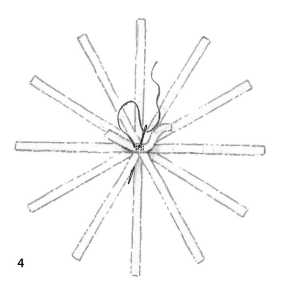

4

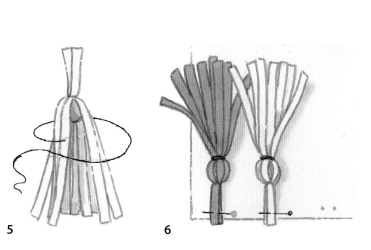

5

6

both long sides. Fold the loops in half end to end, with the seamed sides together, and pin then tack them in the marked positions along the top of the wall hanging, with the fold of the loop facing downwards and the ends aligning with the top edge of the wall hanging (**see picture 3**). Machine stitch in place.

TASSELS Lay one of the tassel hanging loops centrally on top of one of the strips, aligning the long edges. Machine stitch several times across the width to join the pieces together. Lay the other five tassel strips flat, with the strip with the loop on top, crossing them in the centre and fanning out the ends to form an even circle. Pin and tack the centre point through all the layers to keep the pieces in place (**see picture 4**).

Turn the tassel over and place a bead in the centre. Bring all the tassel strips over the bead and wind several strands of matching embroidery thread tightly around them to hold the bead in place (**see picture 5**). Secure the ends of the threads with a few stitches. Repeat to make a total of 15 tassels.

Pin and tack the tassels in the marked positions along the bottom of the wall-hanging front, facing upwards and alternating colours (**see picture 6**). Machine stitch in place along the bottom edge.

LINING With right sides facing, pin and tack the wall-hanging front to the cotton lining. Machine stitch with a 1cm (½in) seam allowance all round, but leaving a gap of approximately 20cm (8in) on one side to turn the wall hanging through to the right side.

Trim the corners to reduce bulk and turn it through, pushing out the corners neatly. Iron the back of the wall hanging. Turn in the seam allowance at the opening and press, then pin and tack

in place. Machine stitch all around the edge of the wall hanging, then stitch a second parallel row 1cm (½in) in from the edge.

EMBROIDERY Work blanket stitch all around the edge using six strands of black embroidery thread. Use the machine-stitched line as a guide and space the stitches 1cm (½in) apart.

Finishing

Lightly press the finished wall hanging with a slightly damp cloth between the fabric and the iron to prevent it from becoming shiny.

Slide the dowel through the loops. Tie the ribbon onto the ends of the dowel and hang the wall hanging from a nail or hook.

Lobster Apron

Inspiration this time has come from wonderful times spent on Martha's Vineyard and Nantucket off the east coast of America, sometimes waiting for a ferry in a harbourside restaurant. This striking lobster design would look very cool enlarged and stitched onto a white linen beach bag.

Embroidery stitches

Blanket stitch appliqué (see page 140), French knots (see page 142), zigzag chain stitch and chain stitch (see page 141).

Preparation

Wash the white and orange fabrics and iron them while still damp to reduce shrinkage (see tips on page 105).

Using a photocopier, enlarge the apron pattern by 400 per cent. Enlarge the lobster design template by 200 per cent.

TRACING THE DESIGN When the design is not symmetrical, as here, it needs to be traced in reverse before being traced through the bonding web, or the motif will appear the other way around on the finished apron. Using a sharp pencil and tracing paper, trace the full-size lobster motif in reverse onto a sheet of paper.

CUTTING OUT Referring to the notes on cutting out on page 106, cut out the apron and facing in the white fabric. Cut out the contrast band for the bottom of the apron in the orange fabric.

Cut out one pocket measuring 41.5 x 22cm (18 x 8¾in) in the white fabric.

Cut out two waist ties measuring 100 x 9cm (39½ x 3½in) and one neckband measuring 58 x 9cm (23 x 3½in) in the orange fabric.

Appliqué

Following the bonding-web instructions for the Love Throw (see page 12), trace the outline of the reversed lobster onto the bonding web using a sharp pencil (**see picture 1**).

Materials and equipment

80cm (31½in) of white linen or cotton fabric (minimum width 110cm/43in) for the apron

60cm (23½in) of orange linen or cotton fabric (dyefast, minimum width 110cm/43in) for the contrast band, neckband, waist ties and lobster appliqué

30 x 20cm (12 x 8in) of bonding web

Apron pattern (page 138)

Lobster design template (page 138)

20cm (8in) embroidery ring

Sharp, hard pencil

Tracing paper and sheet of paper

Dressmaker's carbon paper

Masking tape

Embroidery kit and stranded cotton embroidery thread (dyefast) in black

Sewing machine, matching thread and sewing kit

Iron and ironing cloth

1

2

Iron the bonding web with the lobster marked on it onto the wrong side of the orange fabric and carefully cut out the shape.

Peel off the bonding-web backing and pin the lobster into position, right sides up, on the front bodice of the apron **(see picture 2)**. Using an ironing cloth between the hot iron and the fabric to protect it, iron to fuse the pieces in place.

EMBROIDERY Using dressmaker's carbon paper between the fabric and the template (see page 106), trace over the details of the lobster design to transfer them onto the appliqué shape.

As the detail is quite intricate, secure the fabric in an embroidery ring to work the embroidery and move it over the lobster appliqué as you work. Using four strands of black embroidery thread, work blanket stitch around the body of the lobster, making small stitches 5mm (¼in) long and spacing them 5mm (¼in) apart **(see picture 3)**.

Using two strands of black embroidery thread, work zigzag chain stitch around the legs.

For the inner detail, work zigzag chain stitch using two strands of black embroidery thread.

Using three strands of black embroidery thread, work chain stitch for the antennae.

Finish with French knots for the eyes, using four strands of black embroidery thread, and for the spots, using two strands of black embroidery thread.

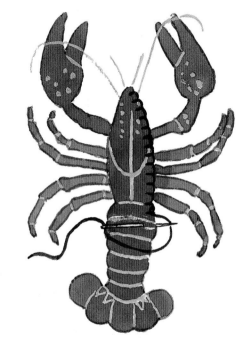

3

When the embroidery is complete, press from the back lightly, taking care not to flatten the French knots (see page 107).

Making up the apron

POCKET Referring to the instructions and picture 2 for the Five-Star Apron on page 64, first hem the top edge of the pocket and attach it to the front of the apron, as indicated on the pattern.

CONTRAST BAND With right sides facing, pin, tack and machine stitch the bottom edge of the apron to the contrast band. Sew the two raw edges together using the zigzag stitch on the sewing machine or overlock, if possible, with a sewing machine that overlocks edges. Press the seam upwards and machine stitch

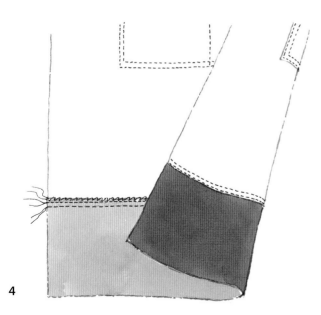

4

a row of topstitching close to the seam on the white fabric. Machine stitch another row of topstitching parallel to this, 8mm (³/₈in) apart **(see picture 4)**.

NECKBAND AND WAIST TIES Follow the instructions and pictures 3–6 for the Five-Star Apron on pages 64–5 to make up and attach the contrast neckband and waist ties, to attach the neck facing and to hem the sides and bottom of the apron.

Note: Make sure you thread the sewing machine with matching orange thread to sew up the neckband and waist ties and to hem the sides and bottom of the contrast band.

Finishing

Press the finished apron on the reverse side (see notes on pressing and finishing on page 107).

Pop Art Quilt

This magical quilt has been made by many skilful hands to celebrate the 'grande finale' of this book and all the projects that have been made for it. It is based on the traditions of a friendship quilt, which is usually stitched by a group of friends for a special occasion such as a wedding, with each patch usually being symbolic in some way. Our quilt is meaningful in its own way – the message here is 'love' and 'love stitching'.

Motifs

Included in this quilt are the following designs:

Pink patches

Love cream appliqué, reproduce letters, page 111, as follows: L at 200 per cent, O at 270 per cent, V and E at 230 per cent; reproduce words, pages 109–10, at 50 per cent, and heart, page 109, at 25 per cent

Heart cream appliqué, page 109, reproduce at 150 per cent

Butterfly black, red and cream design, page 119, reproduce at 250 per cent

Cream patches

Heart pink appliqué, page 109, reproduce at 150 per cent

Galleon black and cream design, page 134, reproduce at 200 per cent

Lips red appliqué, page 112, reproduce at 200 per cent

Multi-Heart red, pink and grey appliqué, page 117, reproduce at 70 per cent

Stars & Stripes Heart red and grey appliqué, page 128, reproduce at 200 per cent

Lobster orange appliqué, page 138, reproduce at 250 per cent

Ladybird red and black appliqué, page 118, reproduce at 400 per cent

Anchor black appliqué, page 136, reproduce at 350 per cent

Red patches

Five Stars cream appliqué, page 125, reproduce at 150 per cent

Tricolour flag red, grey and cream design (two side strips, 38 x 13.6cm (15 x 5½in) and one centre strip 38 x 14.6cm (15 x 6in)

Materials and equipment

Finished quilt size: 199 x 238.25cm (79 x 94½in)

Two pieces of natural linen, 103.5 x 244.25cm (41½ x 97½in) for the backing (including all hem allowances)

30 patches, 38 x 38cm (15 x 15in) in four colours – pink, cream, red and black

Several pieces of bonding web for the appliqué motifs, as required

Motif design templates, as required (see pages 108–38), resized to fit inside the individual patches (see details, left)

Patch pattern (see page 139)

Sharp, hard pencil

Tailor's chalk or marker pen

Metal ruler

Dressmaker's carbon paper

Masking tape

Embroidery kit and stranded cotton embroidery thread (dyefast) in black, pink, orange and cream (plus other colours depending upon the motifs chosen)

Sewing machine, matching thread and sewing kit

Iron and ironing cloth

Je t'aime cream appliqué, page 113, reproduce at 200 per cent

Love cream appliqué, reproduce letters, page 111, as follows: L at 200 per cent, O at 270 per cent, V and E at 230 per cent; reproduce words, pages 109–10, at 50 per cent, and heart, page 109, at 25 per cent

Heart cream appliqué, page 109, reproduce at 150 per cent

Black patches

Psychedelic Flowers pink, green, blue, orange, yellow appliqué, pages 120–3, reproduce at 270 per cent

Union Flag black, red, cream appliqué, page 114, reproduce at 250 per cent and cut square

Crab orange appliqué, page 132, reproduce at 200 per cent

Daisy yellow and pink appliqué, page 124, reproduce at 150 per cent

Heart pink appliqué, page 109, reproduce at 150 per cent

Floral Love red appliqué, page 111, reproduce at 270 per cent

Embroidery stitches

Blanket stitch appliqué (see page 140) for the patches and all the other stitches as described for the individual motifs (see pages 140–3).

Preparation

Plan your design to incorporate your favourite motifs and choose the colour combinations carefully. This quilt uses five 38 x 38cm (15 x 15in) patches in width and six in length to give a finished measurement of 199 x 238.25cm (79 x 94½in). Prepare the linen and wool felt fabrics by pressing (see tips on page 105).

Using a photocopier, enlarge or reduce the chosen motif design templates, as indicated above. Enlarge the patch pattern by 200 per cent.

CUTTING OUT Referring to the notes on cutting out on page 106, cut out the required number of patches in each colour of wool felt. When an embroidery ring is required for the more detailed motifs, cut out 50cm (20in) squares to allow for it. Once the embroidery is complete, use the patch pattern to cut out the patch.

Cut out the backing for the quilt in natural linen. Depending on the size of your quilt, this will probably have to be cut out in two pieces, as here, of 103.5 x 244.25cm (41½ x 97½in), and be joined together by a vertical seam of 1cm (½in), which should fall in the centre of the third column of patches.

Appliqué and embroidery

Use dressmaker's carbon paper (see page 106) to transfer the chosen designs onto the individual patches, remembering to trace them in reverse first if the design is asymmetrical and they have been printed the right way round.

Refer to the instructions in the relevant projects and work the appliqué and embroidery as instructed.

When the embroidery on each patch is complete, press it lightly from the back (see page 107).

Making up the quilt

When all the patches are ready, press the linen backing and lay it on the floor right side up.

Place the patches, right side up, in position on the backing fabric, five across and six down with 1.25cm (½in) gaps between them, starting 5cm (2½in) in from the edges to allow for the hem (see picture 1).

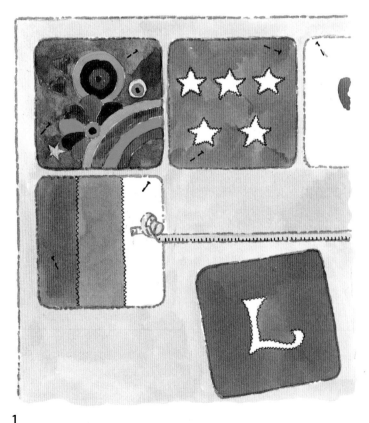

1

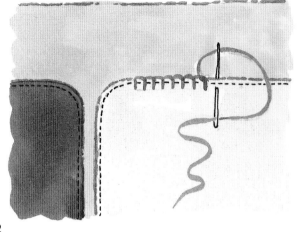

2

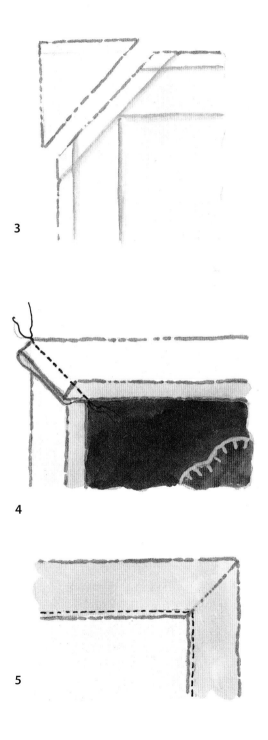

3

4

5

Play around with the positions of the patches until you are happy with the combinations and balance of colours. Pin and tack the patches in place, then machine stitch around the edge of each patch, sewing close to the edge.

Work blanket stitch around the edge of each patch using six strands of embroidery thread in a contrasting colour. Sew even stitches 8mm (³/₈in) long and space them 8mm (³/₈in) apart **(see picture 2)**.

BORDER To hem the quilt and mitre the corners, first fold and press the edge of the linen border 1cm (½in) to the wrong side. Then fold and press the edges 2cm (¾in) to the right side. Bring the fabric together at the corners, making sure the two sides join snugly with no gap, and mark this line diagonally from the corner with tailor's chalk or a fabric marker pen on both sides of the join. Open out the folds and, leaving a 1cm (½in) seam allowance, cut away the corner of the fabric on the diagonal **(see picture 3)**.

Refold the fabric as above and pin, tack and machine stitch the corner seams with right sides together **(see picture 4)**. Press the seam open and turn the mitred corner through. Pin, tack and machine stitch all round the edges on the wrong side of the quilt to form the 2cm- (¾in-) wide hem **(see picture 5)**.

Finishing

Lightly press the edges of the quilt with the tip of the iron and press the embroidered patches with a slightly damp cloth between the fabric and the hot iron to prevent it from becoming shiny.

Tips – before you start

- Always use the best-quality fabrics you can afford, so that the finished embroidered item will last. Traditionally, linen has been the choice of most embroiderers, as it is strong and keeps its shape. I have used good-quality woven wool with a felted finish or natural linen for most projects, and a plain cotton, mainly as a lining.

- If you are not an experienced embroiderer, start off with simple projects that are within your capabilities and learn how to handle the fabric and thread and execute neat, even stitches. When you have gained confidence in your skills, move on to something a little more challenging.

- Before cutting out, if you are using wool and other fabrics that are not washable, prepare them for embroidery by pressing them well with a cloth placed between the iron and the fabric to prevent the hot iron from making the fabric shiny. Dry-clean, if necessary, once the project is complete. For other fabrics, particularly washable ones such as cotton and linen, wash and iron the fabric to ensure that it will not shrink later and ruin the embroidery. This prevents both the embroidery and the seams from puckering if more than one type of fabric is used together.

Embroidery kit

- Embroidery needles
- Stranded cotton thread in the required colours
- Small, sharp embroidery scissors
- Embroidery rings/hoops in various sizes or an embroidery frame

Bonding web

This magical product is used throughout the book for appliqué embroidery. It bonds the appliqué shape securely onto the backing fabric, making easy work of the stitching. Using a sharp pencil, trace the design through onto the smooth side of the bonding web. Iron the bonding web onto the wrong side of the appliqué fabric and cut out the shape, cutting on the inside of the traced outline. Peel off the backing and place the shape in the correct position on the base fabric and pin it in place. Press to seal the shape into position, using a cotton cloth to protect the fabric, if necessary, and remove the pins. The shape is now firmly fused in position and can be placed into an embroidery ring/hoop to be embroidered.

Please note that if the design in the book is not symmetrical, and hasn't been printed in reverse, it will need to be transferred onto the bonding web in reverse. Do this by tracing with your pencil onto the opposite side (the side with the glue) of the bonding web, or use tracing paper and another sheet of paper.

Needles

A chenille needle, which has a large eye to take thicker thread, should be used for the thicker woollen appliqué projects. A fine crewel needle, which has a sharp point and a long eye, is needed for all the projects that are made up with linen and cotton fabrics. Use what you feel comfortable with and, if you can get used to it, work with a thimble to protect your fingers. Needles are graded (1–10) from coarse to fine: the larger the number, the finer the needle.

Threads

Use the stranded cotton variety of thread, which is made up of six strands that can be divided up to give a finer thread. Work with lengths of no more than about 40cm (16in) to avoid the thread tangling and to stop it from losing its sheen.

Embroidery rings/hoops and frames

Embroidery is easier to handle and the results will be more regular if it is stitched in a ring or a frame; there is also less distortion of the fabric. If you are stitching a large piece of embroidery, it is quite easy to move the ring along the piece once a part of the work has been completed. If the project is very large, then a frame can be used, which can be made by joining four wooden battens at the corners; the fabric can be attached with drawing pins or staples. When using a ring, adjust the screw on the outer ring so that it fits snugly over the inner ring and fabric. Ease it down over the inner ring, pulling the fabric taut and removing any wrinkles. Tighten the screw with a screwdriver.

Sewing kit

- Regular sewing needle
- Cotton sewing threads
- Dressmaker's pins
- Scissors for paper
- Sharp dressmaker's shears (use to cut fabric only)
- Tape measure and metal ruler
- Tailor's chalk or water-soluble pen or pencil
- Sewing machine
- Selection of sewing machine needles suitable for heavy and fine fabric
- Iron and ironing board
- Ironing cloth
- Water spray to dampen cloth

Resizing patterns and templates

Many of the patterns and design templates for the projects in this book are shown at a percentage of their actual size. The easiest way to enlarge them to full size is on a photocopier. You may need to tape several pieces of paper together for the larger designs.

Cutting out

- Dressmaker's shears (use to cut fabric only)
- Scissors for paper
- Pins
- Tailor's chalk
- Ruler and tape measure

Make sure that the fabric is crease-free and place it on a large, smooth, flat surface. The true grain of wool, linen and cotton fabric runs down the length, parallel with the edges (selvedges). When placing your pattern onto the fabric, always ensure that the grain line on the pattern is absolutely straight with the grain of the fabric, otherwise the finished item will appear twisted and

hang very badly. If you are using the full width of the cloth (for items such as throws and tablecloths), ensure that the selvedges are neatly cut away first, as these are often stretched and have pin holes in them, which are unsightly and unworkable.

Pin the pattern in place on the fabric and, using tailor's chalk, trace neatly round each piece, checking that the straight grain line is still parallel with the selvedge. Remove the pins and the pattern to reveal the marked shapes. Cut round the shapes with sharp dressmaker's scissors, just on the inside of the chalk line. It is helpful to look ahead at the line as you cut, to produce more accurately cut pieces.

On some patterns there are balance points. These guides require a 5mm (¼in) snip to be made at right angles into the edge of the cloth. Alternatively, mark a dot on the wrong side of the fabric.

If the pattern reads 'cut 2 to pair', cut out one using the pattern the right way up, then turn the pattern over so that it is the wrong way up before cutting out the second. It is necessary to cut fabric to pair when the front of the cloth is different from the back.

Transferring the design

Though there are several methods of transferring the design, the one used throughout this book is with dressmaker's carbon paper. This is available in several colours, so choose one that will show up on the fabric you are using.

Working on a smooth, clean surface, place the carbon paper face down in position on the right side of the fabric and secure it with masking tape. With a sharp, hard pencil, carefully trace around the design, checking to make sure that it is transferring properly.

After the embroidery has been worked, it may be necessary to dry-clean the wool felt or wash the linen or cotton to remove any remaining visible colour.

Embroidering the design

It is advisable to use a ring while embroidering to keep the work flat and in shape and the stitches neat and even. When not embroidering, remove the work from the ring to avoid distortion.

Start a design in the centre and work from there towards the left and then towards the right. If the embroidery is large, move the ring around on the fabric, as necessary.

Do not use a knot to fasten the thread at the start of your work, as this can appear lumpy and unsightly; instead, sew two or three backstitches in an area that will be covered by embroidery. Alternatively, leave 2cm (¾in) of thread loose at the back and darn this into the embroidery once the work has been completed. To finish, secure the thread at the back with several stitches into an embroidered area, and cut off the thread.

Washing after embroidery

If the embroidered fabric needs to be cleaned when the stitching has been completed, dry-clean any fabrics that are not washable, such as wool. For cotton or linen, wash by hand in warm, soapy water and rinse well. Gently squeeze out the excess water, lay the embroidery face down on a towel and iron, being careful not to scorch it, then leave it to dry.

Pressing finished embroidery

Embroidered fabrics need to be pressed lightly on the back to smooth out the creases and wrinkles that may have been caused by the stitching. Pad out the ironing board with a folded towel and lay the embroidery right side down on it and pull it gently into shape. Cover the embroidery with a damp cotton cloth and go over it lightly with the iron, taking care not to squash any heavily stitched areas or French knots. Allow the embroidery to dry properly before handling.

Making up

A basic sewing machine is required to make nearly all the projects in the book. Most sewing machines have a zigzag stitch option, which is useful to neaten seams unless an overlocker machine is available.

Use a 1cm (½in) seam throughout the projects in the book, unless otherwise specified. Wherever the instructions are to pin, tack and machine stitch, remember to remove all the tacking stitches once the machine stitching has been completed.

Always snip off any corners to reduce bulk before turning through. Similarly, taper away some of the seam allowance if the seam is on a curve, to give a better shape once the fabric is turned right side out.

It may be necessary to use heavy-duty sewing machine needles for the woollen projects due to the number of layers that have to be stitched through.

Where a project is made with two different colours of fabric, and where you are stitching a seam with one colour on top of the other, change the colour of the thread in the bobbin on the sewing machine accordingly.

Making bias strips for piping

To make bias strips, you need a large square of fabric. Fold a straight raw edge parallel to the selvedge to form a triangle. Using tailor's chalk and a long ruler, mark out a series of parallel lines to the required width (3cm/1¼in). Cut out and join the strips end to end to make a long strip, and press the seams flat.

Fold the bias strip in half over the piping cord, and pin, tack and machine stitch to close the strip, encasing the cord snugly.

To secure, place the piping along the seam line, and pin, tack and machine stitch it to one side of the article. When stitching around corners, lift the presser foot of the machine at the corner and swivel the fabric around, then lower the presser foot and carry on stitching the next edge – repeating on all the corners.

Where the piped edges meet, cut down the cord so that the ends butt together. Trim the ends of the fabric strips so that they overlap by 1cm (½in), turning under 1cm (½in) on the visible top strip and tucking the opposite raw edge underneath.

Attach the other side of the article by putting right sides together. Pin, tack and machine stitch, using the line of stitching already sewn to attach the piping as a guide.

Trim the corners and clip the edge of the piping, if necessary, to allow ease. Turn the article right side out and press lightly around the edges with the tip of the iron.

Pressing the finished item

Once an article has been completed, press it to give a neat finish, using the recommended heat setting. For wool, use an ironing cloth between the fabric and the iron to prevent shine on the surface. The finished piece should be laid right side down on an ironing board. Be very careful not to flatten the texture of the embroidery. Use steam or a damp cloth to remove any stubborn creases.

Patterns & Templates

Love Throw

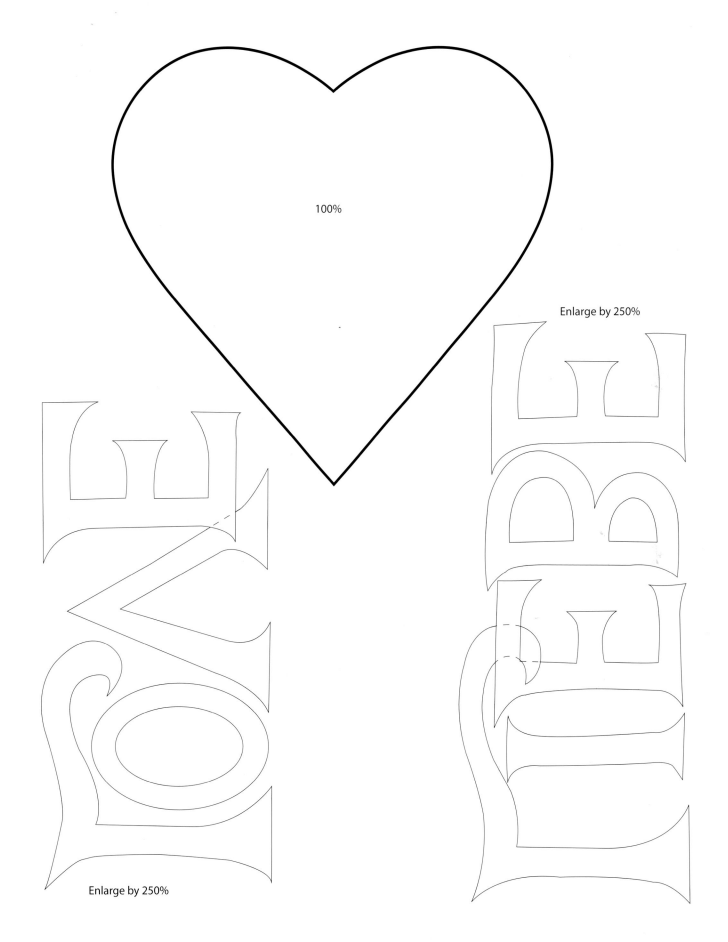

100%

Enlarge by 250%

Enlarge by 250%

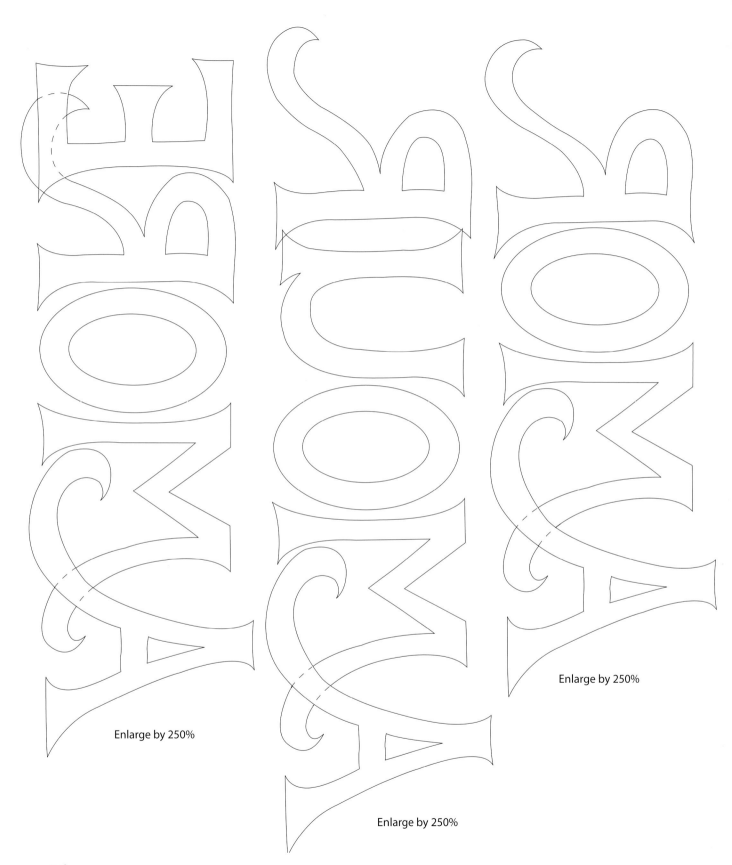

Enlarge by 250%

Enlarge by 250%

Enlarge by 250%

Floral Love Bag   Enlarge by 250%

BAG FRONT AND BACK
Cut 2 in wool felt
Cut 2 in cotton lining

Handle position

Handle position

Lining cutting line

A

B

A

B

100%

Lips Cushion   Enlarge by 220%

CUSHION FRONT
Cut 1 in wool felt

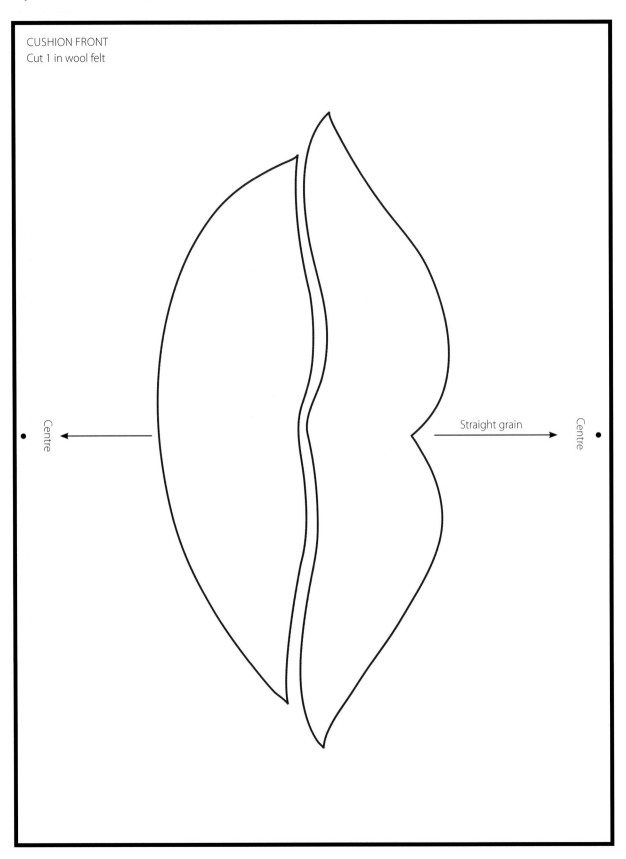

Centre

Straight grain

Centre

Je t'aime Cushion   Enlarge by 220%

CUSHION FRONT
Cut 1 in wool felt

Centre ←

Straight grain →

Centre

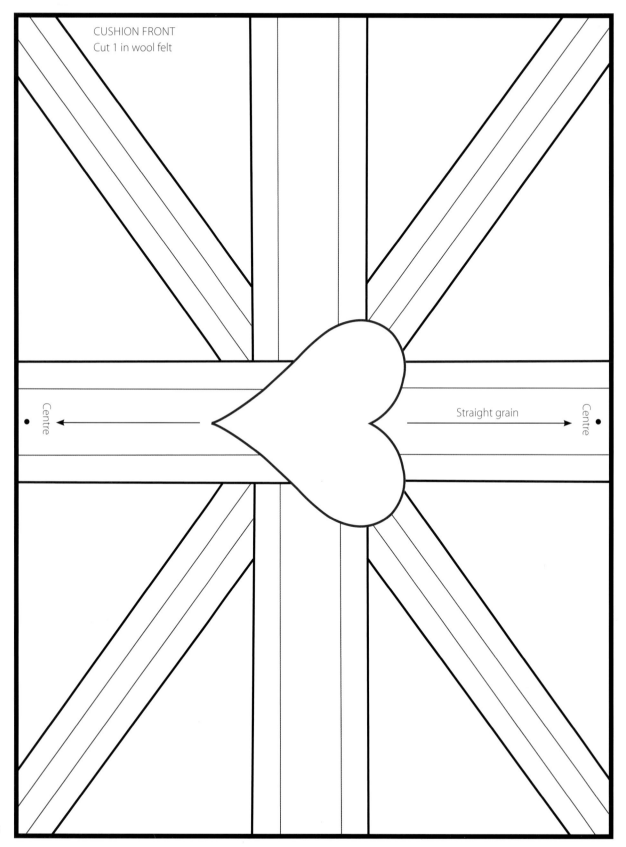

CUSHION FRONT
Cut 1 in wool felt

Centre

Straight grain

Centre

Cushion back for Lips, Je t'aime and Union Flag

Enlarge by 220%

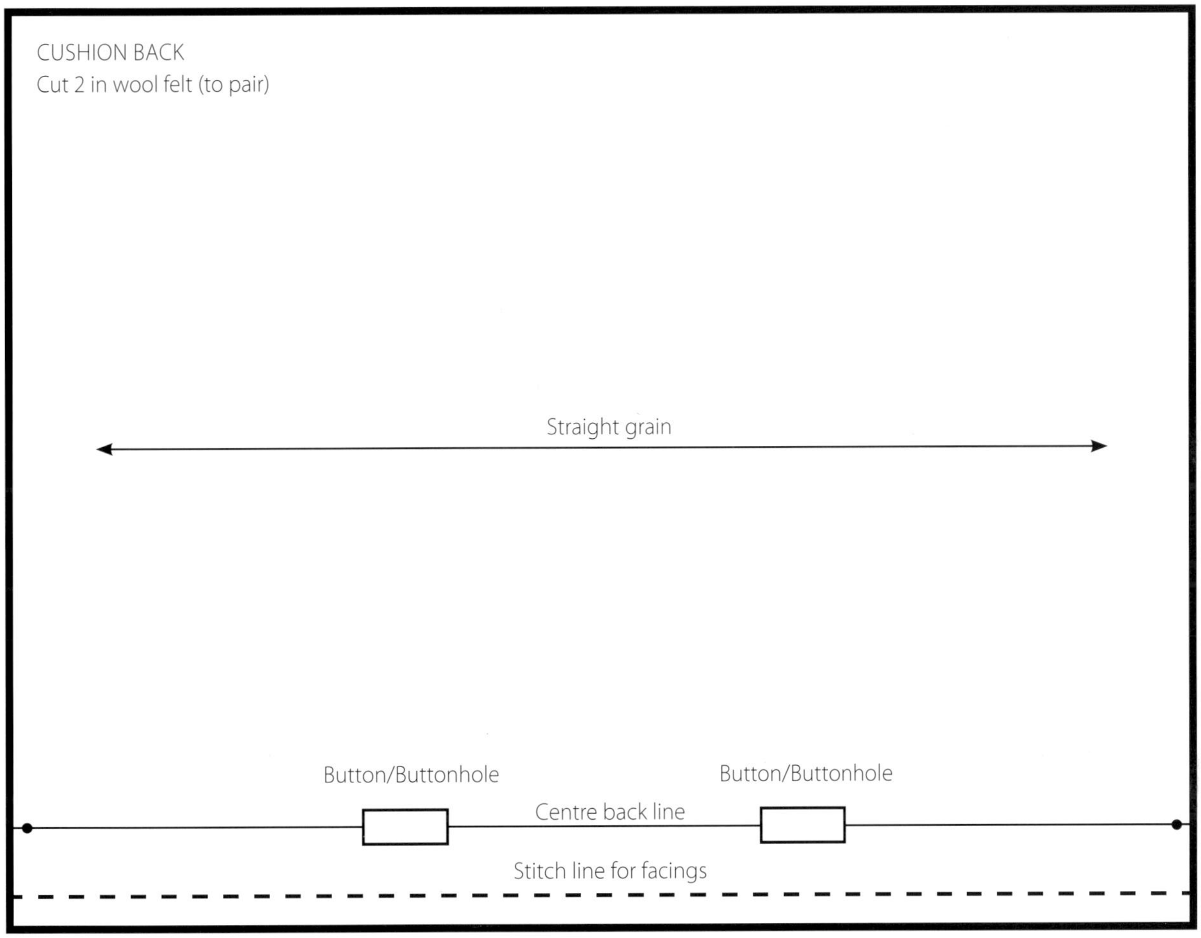

CUSHION BACK
Cut 2 in wool felt (to pair)

Straight grain

Button/Buttonhole   Button/Buttonhole

Centre back line

Stitch line for facings

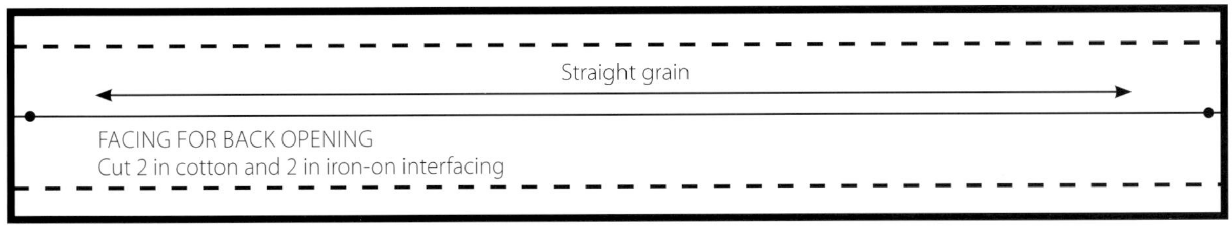

Straight grain

FACING FOR BACK OPENING
Cut 2 in cotton and 2 in iron-on interfacing

Heart Needle Case

Enlarge by 150%

NEEDLE CASE AND LINING
Cut 1 in wool felt. Cut away the inner,
smaller heart from the front cover
Cut 1 in pink cotton lining
Use the outer heart template to
cut out 1 larger heart shape in
contrast wool felt

Ribbon hole

Ribbon hole

INNER PAGES
Cut 1 large and 1 small in wool felt
using pinking shears

Ribbon hole

Ribbon hole

Multi-Heart Rug

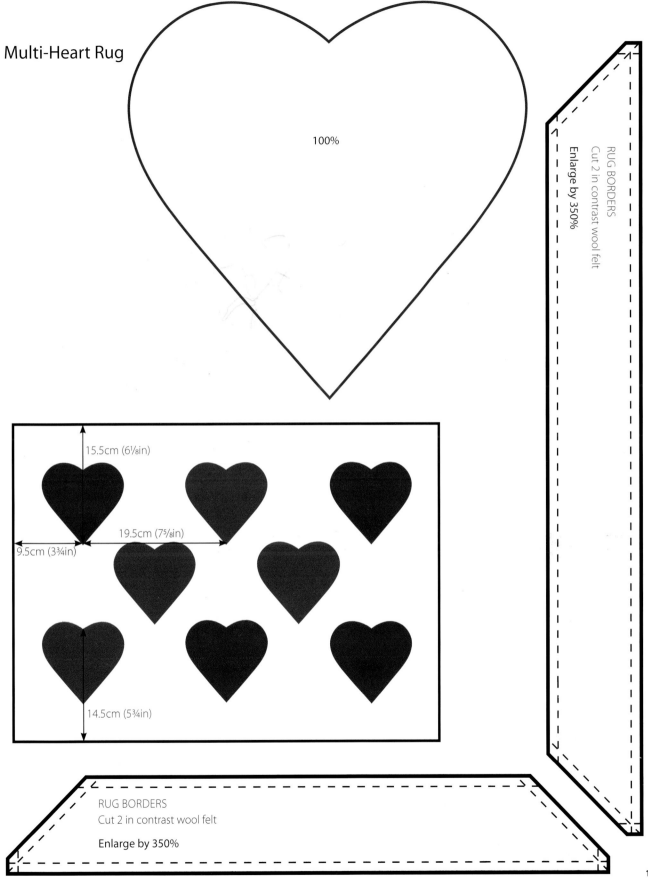

100%

15.5cm (6⅛in)

19.5cm (7⅝in)

9.5cm (3¾in)

14.5cm (5¾in)

RUG BORDERS
Cut 2 in contrast wool felt

Enlarge by 350%

RUG BORDERS
Cut 2 in contrast wool felt

Enlarge by 350%

Ladybird Lavender Heart

Enlarge by 150%

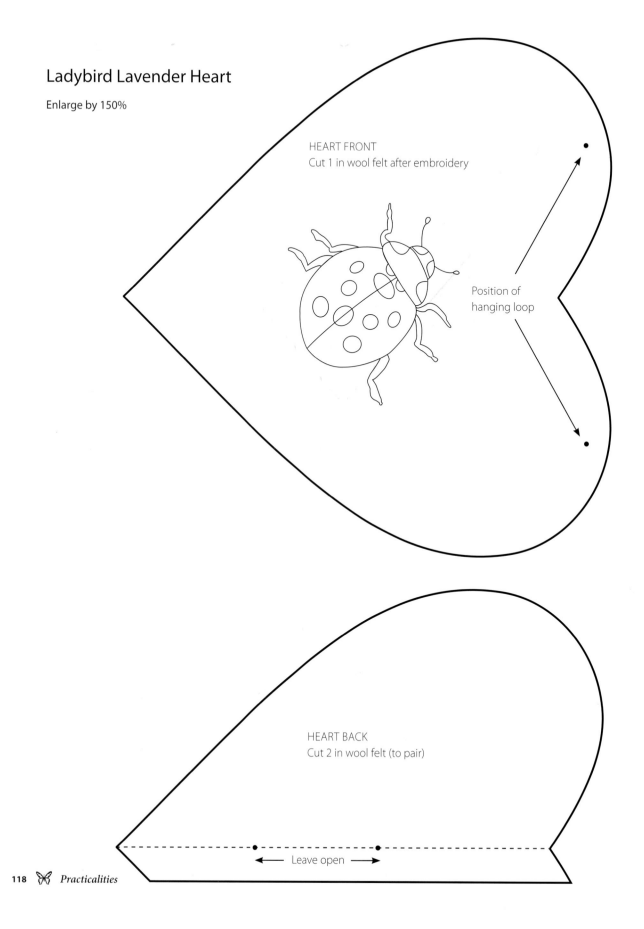

HEART FRONT
Cut 1 in wool felt after embroidery

Position of
hanging loop

HEART BACK
Cut 2 in wool felt (to pair)

← Leave open →

Butterfly Cushion Enlarge by 400%

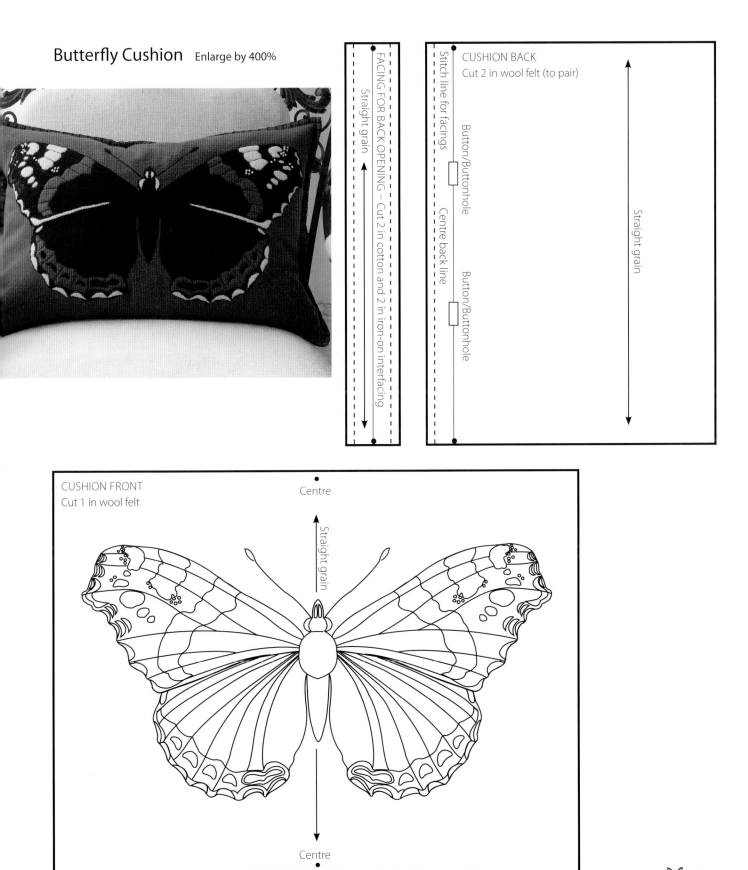

FACING FOR BACK OPENING – Cut 2 in cotton and 2 in iron-on interfacing

Straight grain

CUSHION BACK
Cut 2 in wool felt (to pair)

Stitch line for facings

Button/Buttonhole

Centre back line

Button/Buttonhole

Straight grain

CUSHION FRONT
Cut 1 in wool felt

Centre

Straight grain

Centre

Psychedelic Bag   Enlarge by 250%

Position for zip gusset
and shoulder strap

Position for zip gusset
and shoulder strap

Position of inside pocket on back lining

BAG FRONT AND BACK
Cut 2 in wool felt
Cut 2 in cotton lining

Straight grain

A

B

A

B

Straight grain

ZIP GUSSET
Cut 2 in wool felt
Cut 2 in cotton lining

Enlarge by 250%

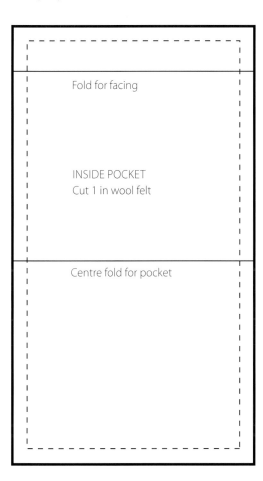

Fold for facing

INSIDE POCKET
Cut 1 in wool felt

Centre fold for pocket

YELLOW APPLIQUÉ DESIGN
ELEMENTS (reversed) **100%**

ORANGE, GREEN, PINK AND BLUE APPLIQUÉ
DESIGN ELEMENTS (reversed) **Enlarge by 150%**

Trace each set of design elements onto a
separate piece of bonding web and fuse with
an iron to the wrong side of the corresponding
coloured pieces of wool felt.

Daisy Make-Up Bag   100%

MAKE-UP BAG FRONT AND BACK
Cut 2 in wool felt

LINING FRONT AND BACK
Cut 2 in cotton lining

Cutting line for bag/fold line for lining

Cutting line for lining

Straight grain

ZIP PULL
Cut daisy outline
after embroidery x 2

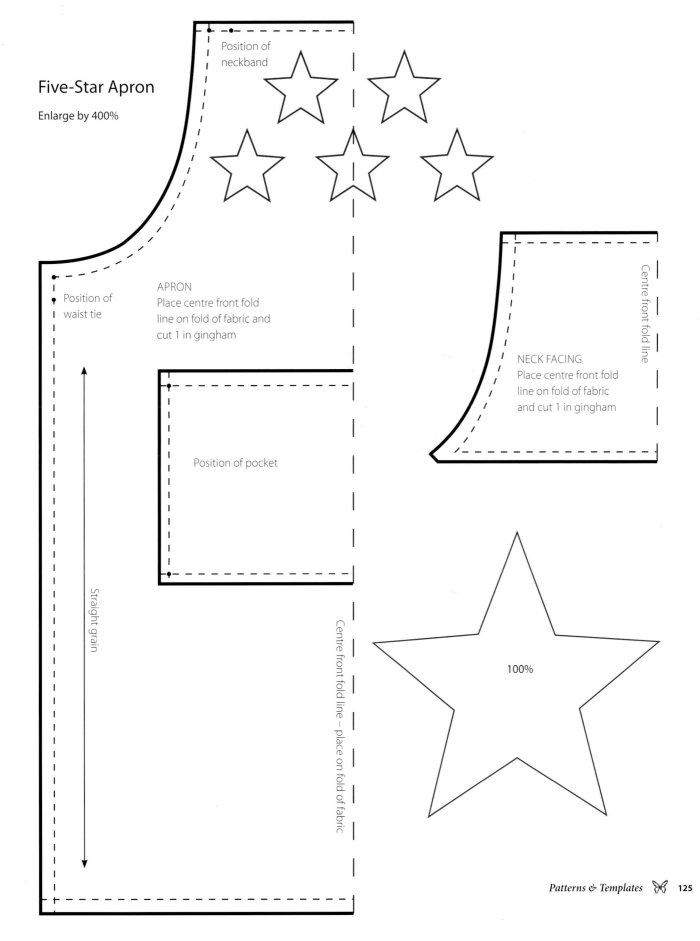

Five-Star Apron

Enlarge by 400%

Position of neckband

Position of waist tie

APRON
Place centre front fold line on fold of fabric and cut 1 in gingham

Straight grain

Position of pocket

Centre front fold line – place on fold of fabric

Centre front fold line

NECK FACING
Place centre front fold line on fold of fabric and cut 1 in gingham

100%

Vintage Rose Cushion

Enlarge by 250%

CUSHION FRONT
Cut 1 in wool felt

Straight grain

Centre

Centre

APPLIQUÉ DESIGN ELEMENTS (reversed) **Enlarge by 200%**

Trace each set of design elements onto a separate piece of
bonding web and fuse with an iron to the wrong side of the
corresponding coloured pieces of wool felt.

GREEN LEAVES

RED ROSES

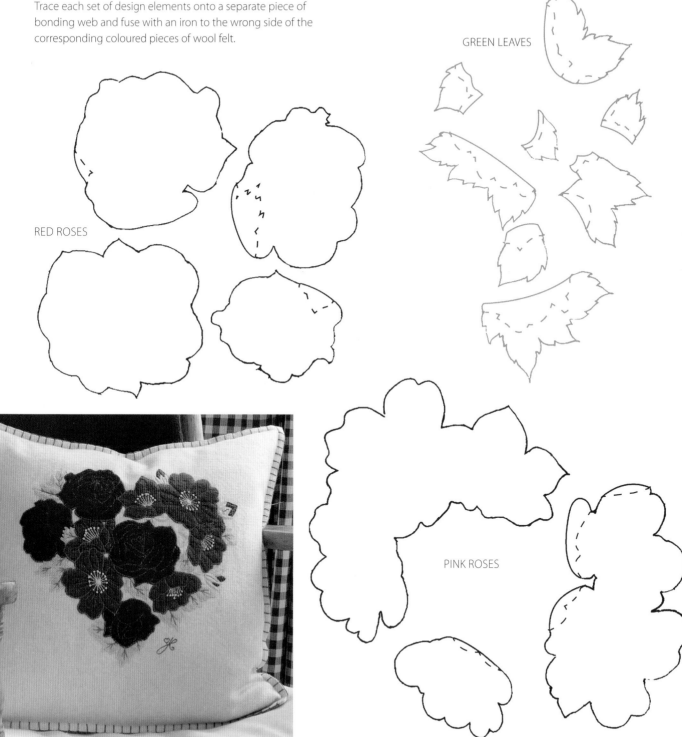

PINK ROSES

Stars & Stripes Heart Cushion

Enlarge by 250%

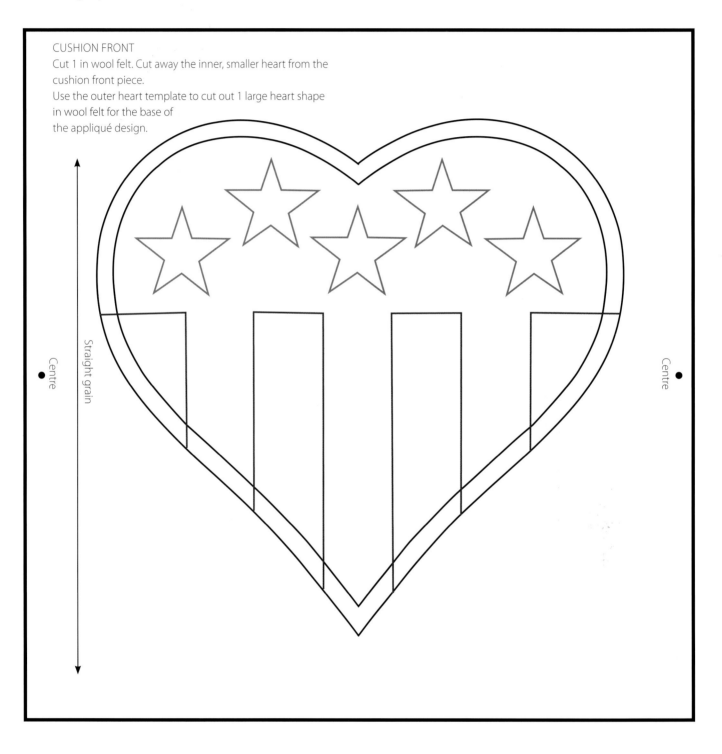

CUSHION FRONT
Cut 1 in wool felt. Cut away the inner, smaller heart from the cushion front piece.
Use the outer heart template to cut out 1 large heart shape in wool felt for the base of the appliqué design.

Straight grain

Centre

Centre

Cushion back for Vintage Rose and Stars & Stripes Heart

Enlarge by 250%

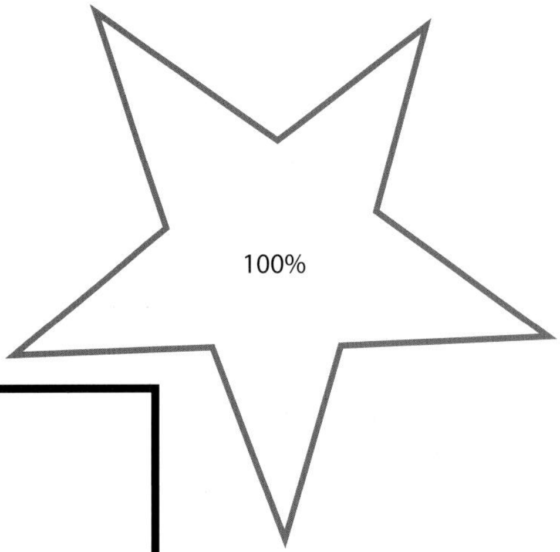

100%

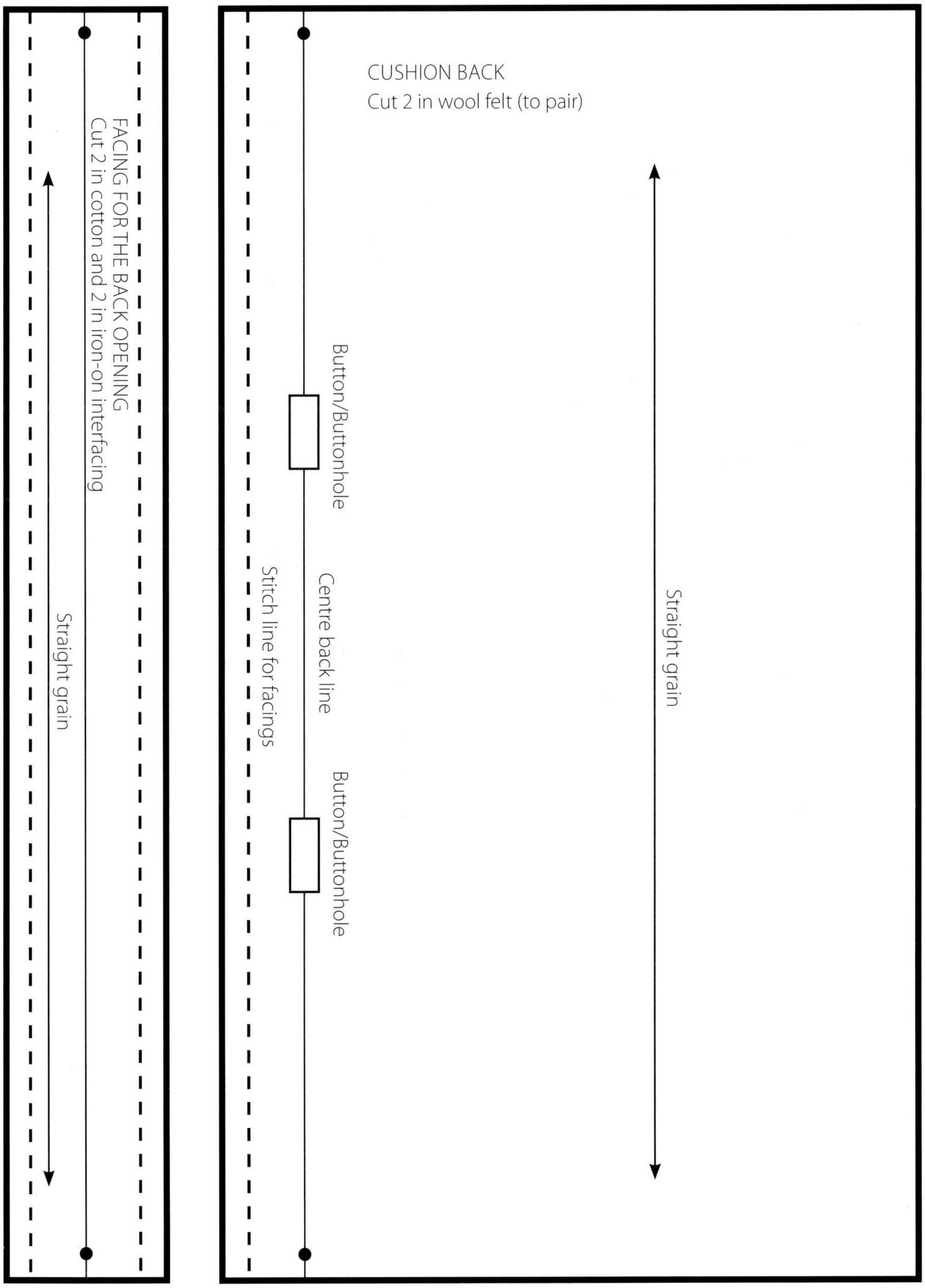

CUSHION BACK
Cut 2 in wool felt (to pair)

FACING FOR THE BACK OPENING
Cut 2 in cotton and 2 in iron-on interfacing

Straight grain

Straight grain

Straight grain

Button/Buttonhole

Centre back line

Stitch line for facings

Button/Buttonhole

Tricolour Flag Bag

Enlarge by 250%

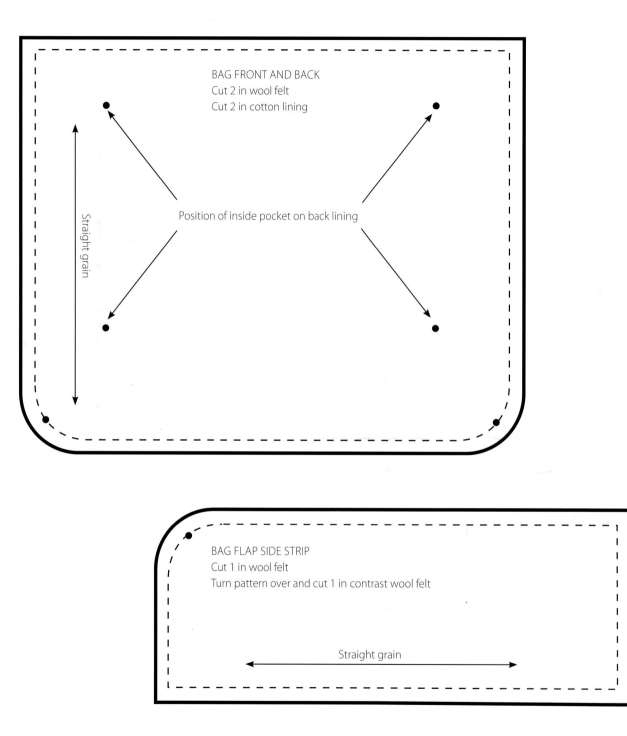

BAG FRONT AND BACK
Cut 2 in wool felt
Cut 2 in cotton lining

Position of inside pocket on back lining

Straight grain

BAG FLAP SIDE STRIP
Cut 1 in wool felt
Turn pattern over and cut 1 in contrast wool felt

Straight grain

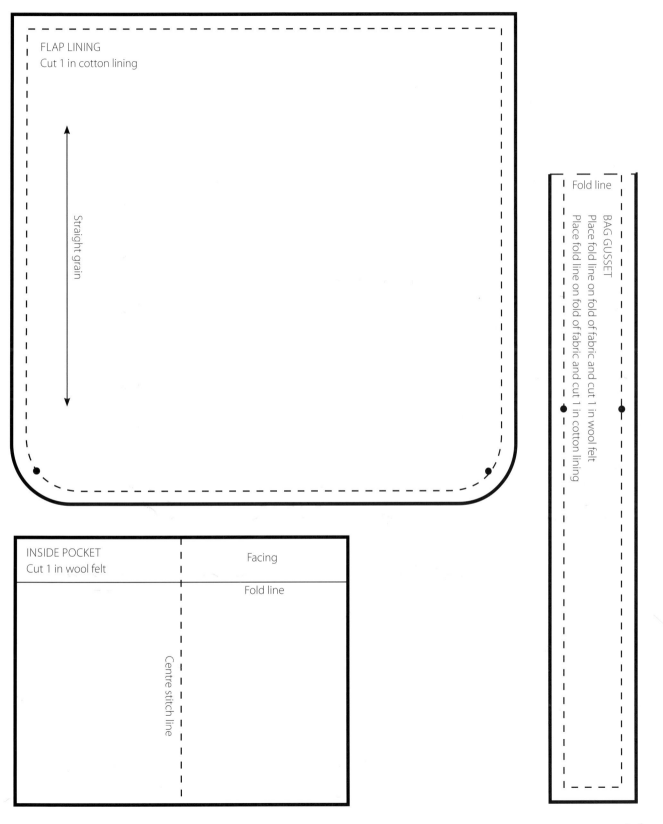

FLAP LINING
Cut 1 in cotton lining

Straight grain

BAG GUSSET
Place fold line on fold of fabric and cut 1 in wool felt
Place fold line on fold of fabric and cut 1 in cotton lining

Fold line

INSIDE POCKET
Cut 1 in wool felt

Facing

Fold line

Centre stitch line

Crab Cushion

Enlarge by 270%

CUSHION FRONT
Cut 1 in linen

Centre

Straight grain

Centre

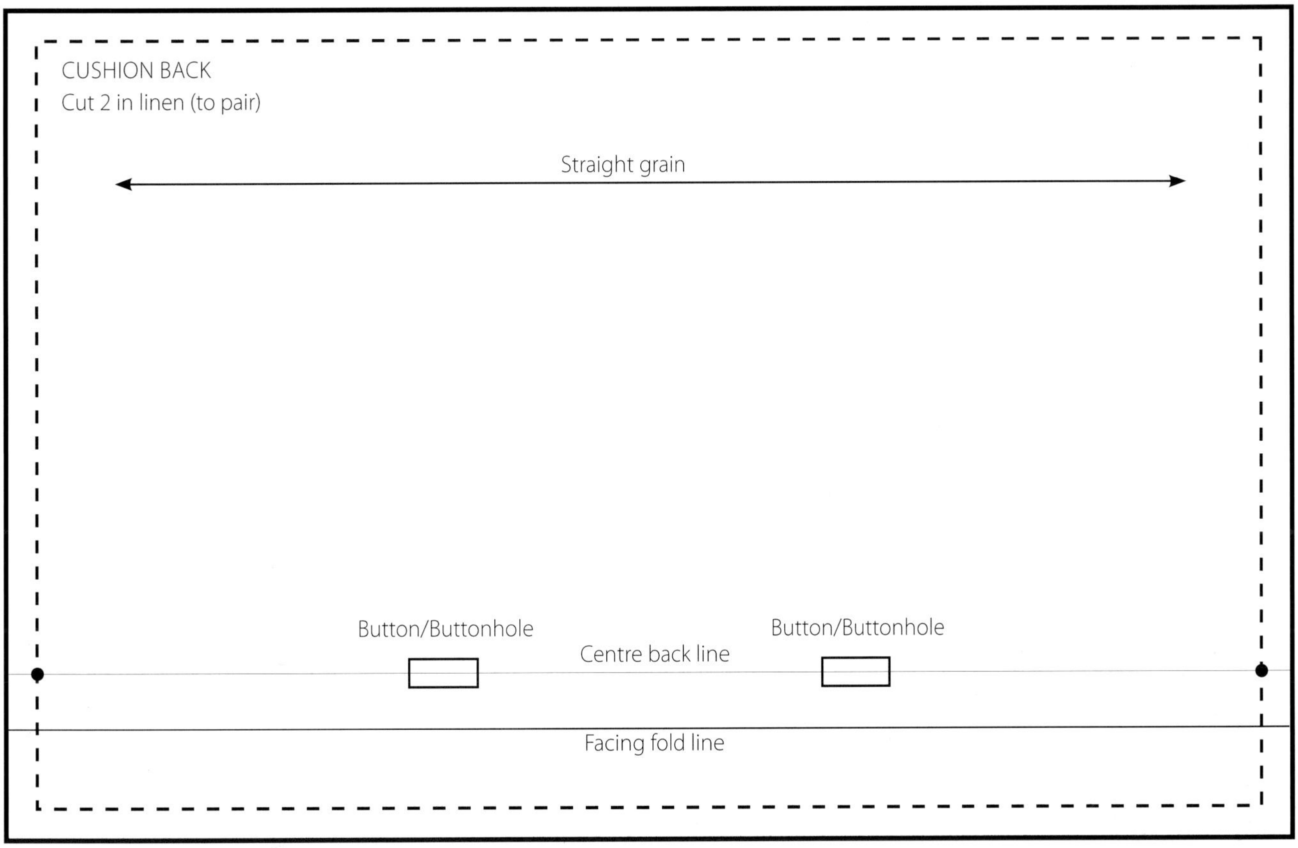

CUSHION BACK
Cut 2 in linen (to pair)

Straight grain

Button/Buttonhole   Button/Buttonhole

Centre back line

Facing fold line

Galleon Wall Hanging   Enlarge by 400%

GALLEON WALL HANGING
Cut 1 in wool felt
Cut 1 in cotton lining

Positions for 5 hanging loops

A Ship is a breath of romance......

Positions for 15 tassels

Flag Placemats

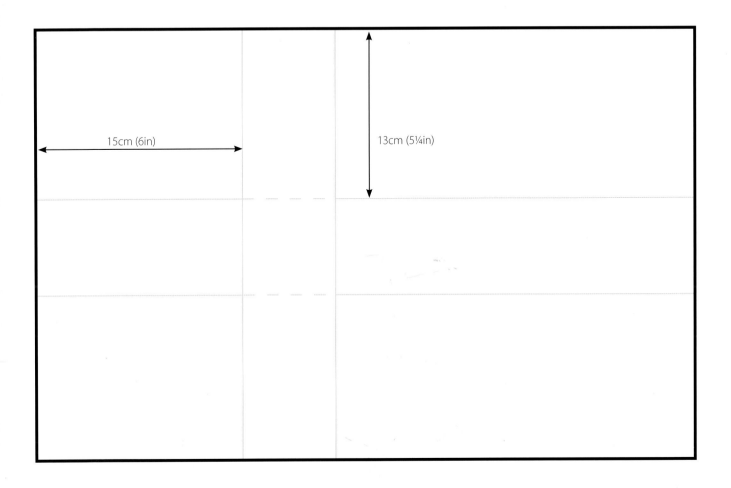

15cm (6in)

13cm (5¼in)

Anchor Seat Pad

Enlarge by 250%

Positions for ties

Positions for ties

SEAT-PAD FRONT
Cut 1 in linen
Cut 1 in wadding/foam

Centre

Centre

Straight grain

Enlarge by 250%

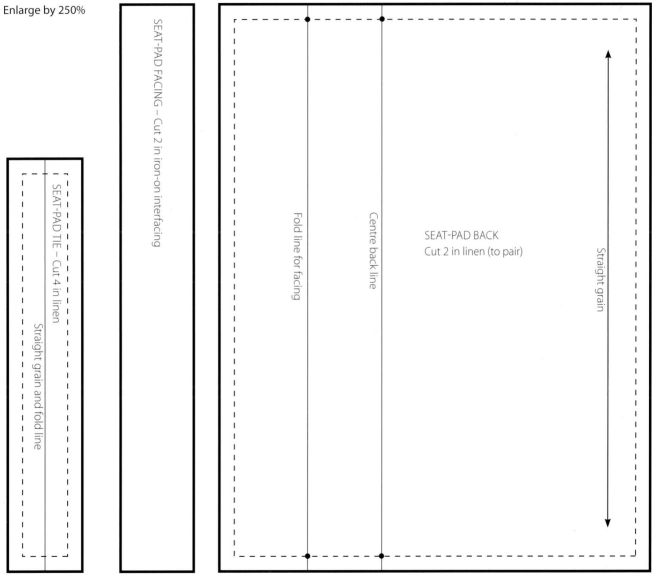

SEAT-PAD FACING – Cut 2 in iron-on interfacing

SEAT-PAD TIE – Cut 4 in linen

Straight grain and fold line

Fold line for facing

Centre back line

SEAT-PAD BACK
Cut 2 in linen (to pair)

Straight grain

Lobster Apron

Enlarge by 400%

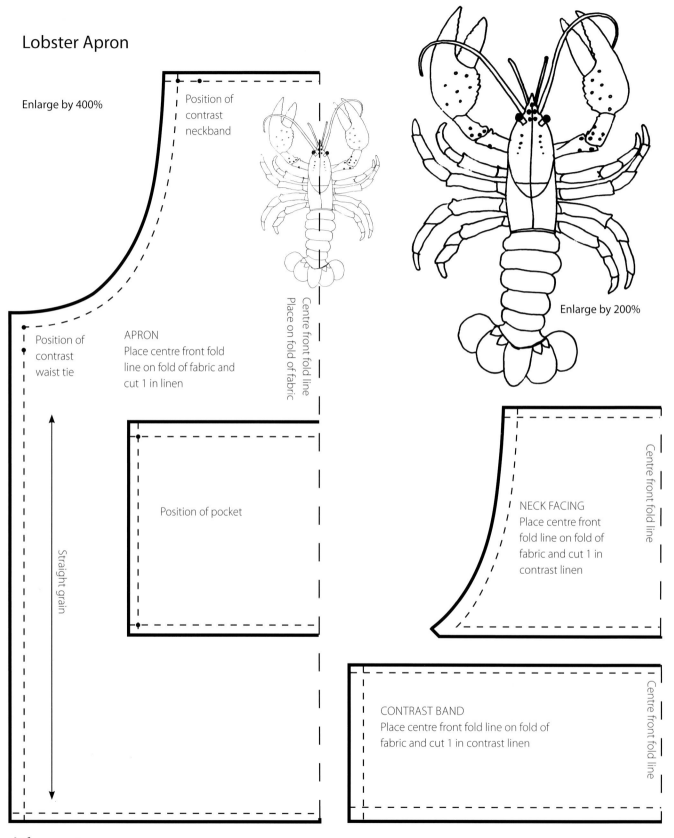

Position of contrast neckband

Position of contrast waist tie

Centre front fold line
Place on fold of fabric

APRON
Place centre front fold line on fold of fabric and cut 1 in linen

Straight grain

Position of pocket

Enlarge by 200%

Centre front fold line

NECK FACING
Place centre front fold line on fold of fabric and cut 1 in contrast linen

Centre front fold line

CONTRAST BAND
Place centre front fold line on fold of fabric and cut 1 in contrast linen

Pop Art Quilt   Enlarge by 200%

QUILT PATCH – 38 x 38cm (15 x 15in)
Cut 30 in wool felt for quilt measuring
199 x 238.25cm (79 x 94½in)

Glossary of Stitches

Blanket stitch appliqué

With the appliqué shape secured in place on the main fabric, either by tacking or bonding web, mark an inner stitch guideline parallel to the edge with tailor's chalk. Working from left to right, bring the needle to the front of the main fabric just below the lower point of the heart, or other appliqué shape. Put the needle back into the appliqué on the upper marked line, one space to the right. Bring the needle straight out again, just below the front edge and over the top of the working thread. Continue as required, spacing the stitches evenly along the row so that they are symmetrical on both sides of the appliqué.

To finish, secure the thread at the back with several stitches into an embroidered area, and cut off the thread.

Blanket stitch edging

This is the traditional stitch used to edge blankets. It gives a neat finish to raw edges and can be used for appliqué. If the vertical stitches are so close that they are touching, it is known as buttonhole stitch.

Using tailor's chalk and a metal ruler, mark a stitch guideline parallel to the edge of the fabric. Working from left to right, bring the needle out to the front of the fabric very close to the edge. Put the needle back in on the upper line, one space to the right, and bring it through to the front again with the tip of the needle over the top of the working thread. Continue as required, spacing the stitches evenly along the row.

To finish, make a tiny stitch on the edge to secure.

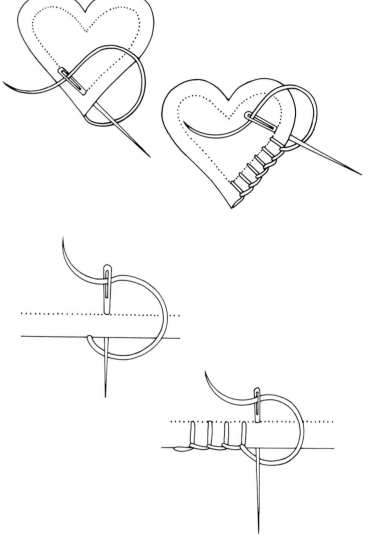

Buttonhole stitch

This is the same as blanket stitch, but with the stitches closer together so that no fabric shows between them. It is used for buttonholes, edging and decorative borders.

To use as an edging, first mark a guideline parallel to the edge of the fabric with tailor's chalk and a metal ruler. Bring the needle out to the front of the fabric on the lower line. Put the needle in on the upper line, slightly to the right, and bring it down and round to the front edge, keeping the working thread under the needle. Continue as required.

To finish, make a tiny stitch on the edge to secure.

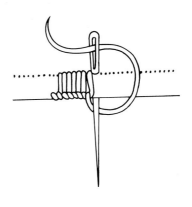

Chain stitch

One of the oldest and most widely used embroidery stitches, chain stitch is used as an outline or a filling stitch by working multiple rows.

Work the chain downwards, making a series of loops the same size and not too tight or they will lose their shape. Bring the needle out to the front of the fabric and return it through the same point, bringing it out again to cover the working thread with the needle, forming a loop. Repeat as required and finish the last loop with a tiny straight stitch.

Zigzag chain stitch

This is a type of chain stitch that, when worked in a straight line, is worked between two parallel lines marked using tailor's chalk and a metal ruler.

Bring the needle to the front of the fabric and then put the needle back in at the same place. Bring the needle back out a little to the left on the opposite line, forming the loop by keeping the working thread under the tip of the needle. Put the needle back in again and then bring it out on the opposite line, a little to the left, forming the loop again. Repeat as required and finish the last loop with a tiny straight stitch.

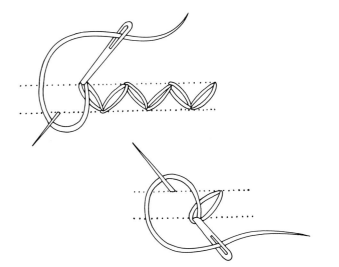

French knot

Bring the thread up through the fabric, hold it with the thumb and first finger of the left hand and turn the needle round it once or twice, or as necessary.

Still holding the thread firmly with the left hand, turn the needle and insert it close to the point at which it emerged (not exactly the same place or it will just pull back through). Pull the thread taut so that the knot slides down the needle to touch the fabric. Release the thread as the needle goes through the fabric with the knot remaining on the surface.

To finish, secure the thread at the back with several stitches into an embroidered area, and cut off the thread.

Cross stitch

Cross stitch is one of the oldest and best-known embroidery stitches. It is quick to do and very effective, as long as the stitches all run in the same direction and are the same size.

Mark two parallel lines on the fabric using tailor's chalk and a metal ruler. Bring the needle to the front of the fabric at point A. Put the needle in at point B and bring it out again at point C. Then put the needle in again at point D and bring it out at point E, continuing to the end of the row.

For the top row of stitches that complete the crosses, use the same holes and work back. Bring the needle out on the bottom row at point G and put it in at point D. Continue in this way to finish the row.

To finish, secure the thread at the back with several stitches into an embroidered area, and cut off the thread.

Basic satin stitch

Satin stitch creates a smooth, solid filling for small areas such as flowers and leaves (see opposite, top). The tension must be kept even and the stitches quite short to keep them neat. Work straight stitches close together, taking the needle through the fabric as illustrated. Repeat consistently for a smooth, even finish with no background fabric visible.

To finish, secure the thread at the back with several stitches into an embroidered area, and cut off the thread.

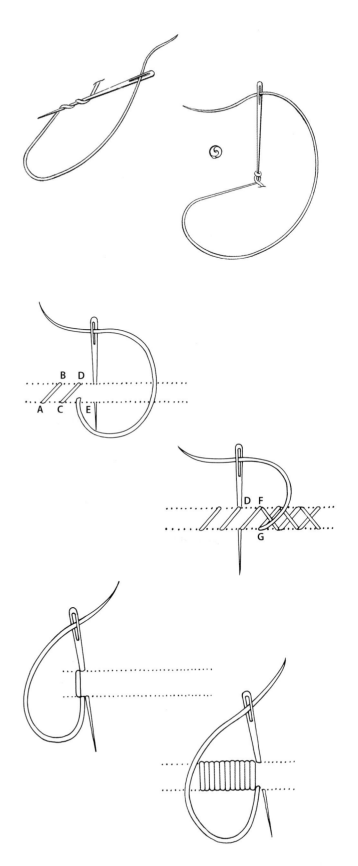

Satin stitch

Work straight stitches next to each other, as described opposite, bottom), but at a slant to suit the shape you are filling. For the bottom part of the leaf, lay the stitches next to each other for a smooth and even finish, with no background fabric visible.

To finish, secure the thread at the back with several stitches into an embroidered area, and cut off the thread.

Closed fly stitch

This is used in the book as a decorative stitch between appliquéd pieces, either in a straight or curved line.

Using tailor's chalk, mark three parallel lines or two lines on either side of a central seam or join.

Working from top to bottom, bring the needle out to the front of the fabric on the middle line at point A.

Put the needle back in at point B and bring it out again at point C, on the left-hand side.

Now put the needle in at point D on the right-hand side and bring it back out at point B, keeping the thread underneath the needle as it comes through to the front.

Spacing the stitches as required, put the needle in at point E, below point B and out at point F, to form the closed fly stitch, and continue on.

To finish, secure the thread at the back with several stitches into an embroidered area, and cut off the thread.

Slip stitch

This is a sewing stitch used for closing a seam. Turn the seams under and press with an iron. Using matching thread and a regular needle, on one side of the opening begin with a stitch that starts from the inside along the folded edge. Cross to the opposite side, stepping back a little, and repeat the stitch. Continue to the end of the seam and secure the thread neatly with a discreet knot.

Directory

Coats Craft UK
Green Lane Mill, Holmfirth, West Yorkshire HD9 2DX
Tel: +44 (0)1484 681881   www.coatscrafts.co.uk
Anchor threads, embroidery equipment, rings and frames, needles,
pins, tracing paper and bonding web.

Ian Mankin
271/273 Wandsworth Bridge Road, Fulham, London SW6 2TX
Tel: +44 (0)20 7722 0997   www.ianmankin.com
Checks, stripes and plain fabrics.

Jan Constantine Ltd
Ravenscroft House, Ravenshall, Betley, Cheshire CW3 9BJ
Tel: +44 (0)1270 821194   www.janconstantine.com
Gingham, ticking fabric, wool felt in all colours, natural linen
and loose aromatic lavender.

John Lewis
300 Oxford Street London W1A 1EX
Tel: +44 (0)20 7629 7711/+44 (0)8456 049 049
www.johnlewis.com
Haberdashery and fabrics of all kinds.

Liberty of London
Regent Street, London W1B 5AH
Tel: +44 (0)20 7734 1234   www.liberty.co.uk
Trimmings, buttons and haberdashery.

V V Rouleaux
102 Marylebone Lane, London W1U 2QD
Tel: +44 (0)20 7224 5179   www.vvrouleaux.com
Ribbons and trimmings.

Whaleys (Bradford Ltd)
Harris Court, Great Horton, Bradford, West Yorkshire BD7 4EQ
Tel: +44 (0)1274 576718   www.whaleys-bradford.ltd.uk
Cotton, linen, silk, wool, wadding and calico fabrics.

Acknowledgements

With love and thanks to all those who have helped me to write this book.

Jacqui Small, for the opportunity to write my second book.

Zia Mattocks, for her great editing and for always being there.

Kate Simunek, for her beautiful paintings.

Barbara Zuñiga, for her wonderful layouts.

Kerenza Swift for all her help and support on the shoot.

Caroline Arber, my outstanding photographer, for her beautiful images full of light and her lovely home as backdrop.

My cherished friend Maggie Martin, for her help throughout.

Jo, for her wonderful sewing and hard work.

Sharon and her skilled artisans, for their beautiful embroidery stitched in impossible time scales.

Sam, for her help on the shoot and other practicalities.

Kim, Diane and Nikki, and all the girls in the office, for holding the fort while I worked on the book.

My husband David, for his total help and support while I worked through Christmas and beyond to reach my deadlines. Also my daughters, Camille and Mary Flora, for being so tolerant.

My sister Elaine, for her generous support.

And, finally, all my friends and family for putting up with me and my ludicrous timetable over the last few months.